THE CARDINAL METHOD OF LIFE CONNECTION

Aligning Consciousness With The Power of Crystals

Paola Novaes Ramos, PhD

© 2017 Paola Novaes Ramos, PhD
All rights reserved.

ISBN: 1548398179
ISBN 13: 9781548398170
Library of Congress Control Number: 2017910136
CreateSpace Independent Publishing Platform
North Charleston, South Carolina

The best of life begins with connection to the real self.

Paola Ranova

Illustrations by Paola Ranova.
As a university professor and educator, I would like this book to be a heart-to-heart with its readers.

I have created the illustrations myself as if they were on a white board in a classroom, and I hope you enjoy them as thousands of students in my career have.

ACKNOWLEDGMENTS

Thanks to all the wonderful people who have supported me in this journey.

To my awesome, loving husband, Ronald Roseo.

To my wonderful parents, Marcus Vinicius and Clarinha Ramos; my brother, Guilherme Ramos and sister-in-law, Dora Ramos, who have always been by my side.

To my cousin Andrea Lafetá, for being the first person to ever tell me about chakras.

To my yoga master, Vilma Arakaki.

To my metaphysics teacher, Alice Schroeder, and my Enneagram guides, Nilda Paes and Angélica Bessa.

To Viviane Ribeiro, for the depth of soul in my transpersonal work.

To Claudia Diégues, Carminha Carvalho, and Ana Paula Faber, for their friendship.

To Natália Lleras, for her wisdom and loving presence, and for introducing me to the work of Jamie Sams.

To my family constellation friends who were first introduced to **The Cardinal Method of Life Connection**, especially my masters, Elizabeth Carneiro and Laura Coutinho; our hosts at Vale da Lua, Mari and Oskar; and all the constellation community that has supported my work in Brasilia.

To Dr. Janet Galipo, Dr. John Veltheim, and Dr. Esther Veltheim for the mentorship and inspiration in the United States.

To Rev. Gisèle King, for her wisdom, loving support, and spiritual guidance.

To my friends Maina Campos, Kuki Alves, Patricia Hoyle, Sonia Terrosa, Su Singh, Ada Dana, Ana Izquierdo, Becca Marshall, and Susan Hally, for their loving and joyful presences.

To the 2 Be Healthy team in Miami—Ivanara Moura, Karen Taylor, Ren Michaeli, Robert Hurley, and Laszlo Thoth—for their love and support to the **CMLC**.

To the BodyTalk community, for their consciousness, strength, and kindness of heart.

To all Ranova clients and the energy healing community of South Florida, for the contribution to the development of **The Cardinal Method of Life Connection** on US soil.

Thank you!

CONTENTS

Acknowledgments		vii
Introduction		xi
1	Understanding Higher Consciousness	1
2	Crystals	29
3	Family Constellations	47
4	Native American Wisdoms	97
5	The Hindu Chakras System	117
6	Individual Aspects of the Psyche	150
7	Aligning Our Inner Worlds with the Power of Crystals	160
References		175

INTRODUCTION

I'm Dr. Paola Novaes Ramos, also known as Paola Ranova, and I am very happy to share **The Cardinal Method of Life Connection** (**CMLC**) with you.

As a comparative studies and multidisciplinary educator and researcher, I present to you the result of twenty-five years of research and observation of human nature, consciousness, and the human experience based on a myriad of inspirations and sources of knowledge.

From age fourteen to age thirty-nine, I have researched and developed the fundamental structures of **The Cardinal Method of Life Connection**, which you now hold in your hands as you read this book. I hope you enjoy the ride and that it brings insight to your personal growth, consciousness expansion, and spiritual connection.

Creation and Development of The Cardinal Method of Life Connection
The **CMLC** is an energy technology modality that uses crystals as tools for consciousness expansion and soul healing. It was created and developed as a synthesis of some of the most important consciousness modalities I have come to know in my life. It integrates

both my academic background and my personal experience in a soul-searching journey since my teenage days.

Professionally, I developed a career as a professor of political theory with a focus on human nature, human consciousness, and moral philosophy, and in parallel I have explored the fields of consciousness and spirituality from a very early age. When I became a teen, I was especially trying to understand how individuals interact with the physical and social world through their different cultural, mental, emotional, and spiritual perspectives.

I found out through many years of research that individual human beings develop such unique, subjective, and independent ways of looking at the world that it can be hard to develop objective thinking and reach consensus about which basic actions we should take to create a happy life, not only for us as individuals, but also for the communities we are immersed in and for humanity.

At the same time, certain aspects of human nature and the human experience are universal, such as the search for love, joy, happiness, peace, personal fulfillment, and belonging. What I found out in more than twenty-five years of research and several spiritual journeys into my inner world is that these all good things can be achieved if we contemplate the truth, get rid of our "spiritual errors," and establish a conscious life connection.

The subject of human nature and consciousness fascinated me so much that I became a PhD in multidisciplinary systems and comparative cultures, and a professor of human nature and moral philosophy within the scope of political theory. As a PhD in multidisciplinary systems and comparative cultures, I have researched a lot of spiritual knowledge and comparative religions in the process of both my academic life and my personal search for happiness and fulfillment. I wanted to understand the myriad of perspectives about life, and as I compared intellectual and spiritual approaches, I created and developed **The Cardinal Method of Life Connection**. This system is not only the result of robust academic research, but also a picture of my personal journey described in this book in its state of art.

Before my personal soul journey started, in my childhood I felt that life was emotionally challenging, because there was so much cruelty, lack of love, and social inequality in the world. Because I was born to such loving, wonderful parents, however, I felt that ultimately life could be good, and strong, and abundant. I refused to believe it was cruel, fearsome, and evil.

As a very young child, life made sense when I was connected to loving human beings, or to nature. All distortions seemed to go away with loving human connections and natural environments. For that awareness, I am grateful to have grown up in Brasilia in the 1980s, where we had lots of natural spaces, trees, open skies, and abundant rainwater and waterfalls. I also had many family members around, which helped to create a loving, supporting environment.

Later in my preteen days, I was especially happy when I found out the city is built on top of a huge quartz crystal shield. That made me feel intuitively safe. And even if I felt safe with my family, the huge quartz crystal and the lush *cerrado* (typical Brazilian savanna) nature, I felt Brasilia was emotionally dense. As the capital of Brazil, it was home to a lot of political and power struggles that deeply affected the emotions and behaviors of the children who were growing up there.

The people who populated the city had recently moved to a new place built in the middle of nowhere, with a lot of hopeful perspectives, but it was still a very bold project. To me, nature seemed wonderful and unknown in the natural *cerrado* lands, and I did have a lot of family members around, but at the same time, life was emotionally bleak in the social and political environment at the time.

This scenario of abundant nature and emotionally detached people raised my interest to see beyond the immediate physical and social world. At a very early age, I wanted to try to find deeper causes and more meaningful reasons for life. In my early teens, the path I chose to make sense of it all was to seek philosophical knowledge and spiritual wisdom. This journey began not only out of curiosity, but mostly from a need to make sense of life and explore its subtle realities.

At age thirteen I started reading about Hindu and Greek philosophy. I was especially fascinated with chakras on one side, and Socrates and Plato on the other. A year later, I began to take yoga classes. Learning about chakras and going to yoga classes with my mother was an amazing experience. She told me she had been taking yoga classes for many years, and that she had started when she was pregnant with me.

That touched my spirit, because I realized yoga felt like home from the womb. In the yoga classes, I began to understand the subtle aspects of human existence through physical sensations in my body. I felt the energetic flow of a very powerful life force intertwined with a receptive state of being in the breathing exercises, the *asanas* (physical postures), and the meditations.

Yoga made it clear to let me that there is something very real beyond our physical bodies. These subtle energies helped me understand that when we are connected to life, everything has meaning and purpose. Life and consciousness unfold in endless possibilities of creativity and fulfillment.

In parallel I was already fascinated with crystals. Soon after that I started researching about their subtle properties, and it was one of the biggest turning points at the time that opened my mind, heart, and soul to the consciousness expansion I was seeking. I realized that both philosophy and spiritual knowledge could be deep and expansive, and that their connection with nature could happen in ways unknown to our Western cultures. It all made sense to my heart, and this interest led me to research many other spiritual traditions and energy modalities from then on.

When I was seventeen, I was fascinated with nature, crystals, chakras, and colors, and I needed to make a choice about college and which career I wanted to lead. I was torn between a visual arts major, because I truly loved illustration, and political science with a focus on human nature and moral philosophy.

I loved both areas but decided I needed to strengthen my left-brain abilities with more in-depth philosophy about human nature. It was the right time to train my brain power, and my love for art could wait. If I dedicated myself to the study of human nature and social interactions, I would be able to create meaningful, fertile things that contemplated both reason and logical thinking, and depth of soul through visceral, natural, artistic, and spiritual expression. I could later use my accumulated academic knowledge to make art. I wanted to create things that would be a complete expression of my fulfilled inner world, and for that I needed to train my brain in logical thinking, since art already flowed so viscerally and instinctively for me.

I became an undergraduate student of political science at the University of Brasilia and continued studying energy and spiritual knowledge to cultivate my passions. I would take personal-growth and spiritual courses on free nights, weekends, and summer breaks. I would also always make time to read and study these wisdoms a few hours a week since I loved it so much, intercalating this material with the body of academic reading I needed to build a solid professional life.

When I was twenty-one and graduating from college, new knowledge about the soul and the self came to my life in an unexpected way, when I learned about the Enneagram. The Enneagram is an ancient spiritual system of self-understanding and soul searching that uses sacred geometry to understand human consciousness. It was part of Pythagorean studies and mystic Sufi tradition, among other traditions. It's interesting how my personal journey has these specific decisive moments—like my discovery of chakras and crystals—in which new spiritual knowledge always comes into my path when I'm taking steps to advance in my academic career. I am starting to get used to this type of synchronicity in specific times of my life.

For five years, I was deeply immersed in the Enneagram literature and Enneagram therapeutic groups and practices in Brasilia. In the meantime, I got married to my first husband, finished my master's degree, and in parallel studied personality structures and virtuous paths in the Enneagram literature, with special focus on the spiritual perspective, and attended the practice workshops.

When I was twenty-seven, a big emotional shift happened as another brand-new spiritual knowledge entered my life. I got accepted as a PhD student at the Center for Studies about the Americas at the same time I was getting divorced from my first husband. That was also exactly when I started studying spiritual knowledge material with a group of powerful women guided by my transpersonal therapist at the time.

I was at a bookstore one day, and a book about spiritual knowledge and personal development literally fell off the shelf and into my hands. On that same week, my therapist called me saying she was starting a new group to study this spiritual knowledge using that exact book, which I had never heard about until that day. I was impressed with the coincidence and immediately immersed myself in the knowledge of energy, consciousness, and spiritual connection for more than four years.

THE CARDINAL METHOD OF LIFE CONNECTION

During my self-healing process as I went through the divorce, and as I tried to heal emotional pain and understand that part of my life path with the help of spiritual knowledge, meditation, and journaling, I was comparing European perspectives and social values and different Native American cultures for my thesis in my PhD program. After I finished the PhD credits, I got a grant to live in Europe for a year to understand traces of rational European culture and values about belonging in Western culture.

I had always wanted to live in Europe, especially Barcelona. When I visited this city as a tourist at age nineteen, I promised myself I would live there someday. And ten years later, there I was.

I did not want to quit my therapeutic sessions and spiritual practice, so I kept in touch with the work of my transpersonal group via the Internet as I traveled to Europe for my research. Since the thesis used comparative studies as a methodology, I was researching the European state model and *Tahuantinsuyu* (the "Inca Empire") in European libraries, as I went to church every day to keep my spiritual focus. The good thing about European cities is that every day you can go to a different church and have not only a spiritual but also a cultural experience.

One day, I was researching about Inca sovereignty as a spiritual empire. I searched the Internet for keywords about blood ties and spiritual connections within families in social organizations, with a focus on different political types of authority. To my absolute surprise, this word search that combined "family blood ties" and "spirituality" led me to a very peculiar concept I had never heard of before: something called "family constellations."

I was in a public library in Barcelona when that happened. When I started reading about this unknown and vast family constellations literature, I was hooked. So much of what I was looking for to understand the Inca Empire was oddly explained in the family constellation literature through concepts such as "unconscious belonging" and "collective soul."

More important than that, however, was that my journey toward spiritual connection was unfolding in deeper levels as my academic research began to merge with spiritual knowledge and therapeutic modalities. I was already familiar with spiritual explanations for the great questions of life, and now they were mingling with my academic researches. It was strange and fascinating to see two separate worlds starting to unintentionally connect so naturally in my path, as I moved forward in my academic and spiritual life simultaneously.

My conscious intention in the academic field was to rationally understand human actions, and at the time I had no idea about what "collective emotional healing" was. It was a new concept for me from family constellations literature, and this idea of "collective soul" and "collective emotional healing" and "unconscious family bonds" kept flashing in my mind—and sometimes even in my sleep.

Even if this search was leading me to themes such as "family bondage" and "emotional healing" beyond the original scope of my academic research for the thesis, which revolved around rational explanations about human experiences in different social organizations, I felt it was all making sense as I saw the big picture. I knew I needed to keep digging more.

As I kept writing my PhD thesis and it led me to research more about the concept of a "shared soul" in a group of people, I began to feel I was literally being guided to merge my academic knowledge with spiritual wisdoms—it was not just a random flow. I had already been researching my inner world and trying to engage in my own personal growth and self-awareness for years, and now I had encountered this knowledge about a new therapeutic modality for the soul.

After my one-year research in Europe was finished, I moved back to Brazil with many ideas to organize and discuss with my fellow researchers at the Center for Comparative Studies about the Americas, as I had to write the thesis and weave together all the knowledge.

One day, I went out to lunch with a friend in Brasilia, and we were talking about many different things and catching up. She told me casually about her two-year-old daughter, who had suddenly become aggressive with her. I could only imagine how a mother would feel when her two-year-old resisted her. My friend said she could not allow that barrier to grow between them, so she went to an individual family constellation session. Of course, I was intrigued, because I had not mentioned family constellations to her at all during our conversation.

My friend went on to tell me that her daughter's behavior changed completely. The little girl went back to being her normal, natural, sweet self again—after just one session.

Now I was more than intrigued. First, I was beginning to understand there are no such things as coincidences. Was I truly experiencing synchronicity, which is a spiritual concept that tells us we are on the right track when we decide to engage in a consciousness path? This was a lawyer friend, whom I had worked with years before at a university center in Brasilia. I had not asked her about family constellations, and she was not part of my spiritual circle of friends. She mentioned the constellation story on her own.

Second, not only did the theory part of family constellations seem very interesting, but now it also seemed like it had had practical—and powerful—results.

I told my friend a little bit about my research and that I had only read about constellation theory. She said I had to talk to the facilitator who gave her the session and see for myself how incredible it was and how it worked. She gave me the number of the facilitator and told me to call her.

I hesitated and said I probably wasn't ready for the practice of constellations. It seemed too intense for me, and before I defended the thesis, I could not focus on anything else. But I said I would call her when the time was right. Today I know I was unconsciously resisting the constellation energy, as I see so many people do unless they are truly desperate. But at the time, my rational excuses all seemed very consistent, so I ignored engaging in my own constellation process and stuck to the theory.

That same week when I had lunch with this friend, I was at my mom's house looking for some of my old books about the national state or some other social science theme. As I was running my fingers through the books on the shelf, what did I find? A book titled *Family Constellations*, by Bert Hellinger.

I remember getting chills. What was going on? I knew enough about synchronicity to pay attention to this unfolding of family constellations in my life. This was no coincidence. Life was clearly telling me to dig deeper, to go in that direction, and I literally kept seeing arrow images pointing in one direction in my mind. Strangely or not, I felt this whole constellation story was not only for personal development, but also for the healing of many—not only in our own families, but also for the communities we are immersed in and probably whole cultures and even all of humanity.

I felt like a grain of sand in an ocean: we are a tiny part of the whole, yet we know that if we shine light within, we are helping the collective unconscious raise its vibrations. Constellation theory kept coming up all the time. I figured this weird movement of focusing and researching for my academic work leading me to more spiritual knowledge had a higher purpose.

When I looked at the Hellinger family constellations book, I was sure it had come to my parents' home through my mom, and not my dad. He is a medical doctor and was never interested in soul healing and energy—on the contrary, he was explicitly skeptical about it. My father has always respected my interest in energy healing and my spiritual practices, but he never wanted to have anything to do with it. I was sure he would not have bought that book. My mom, on the other hand, had always been more open and interested in holistic approaches, so I asked her about it.

She said she had bought it a few years back because this wonderful priest who taught us the Silva Mind Control techniques had suggested it to her, but she had never read it. She just left it on the shelf, and it had been sitting there for years. Without really thinking much, I started reading the book.

I read the whole thing that very night, and I could not sleep. The more I read, the more impressed and even shocked I was, because what Hellinger was saying in those pages was not only life changing, but also a kick in the gut. This was one of his earliest books, and in the initial stages of family constellations, Hellinger could be raw for those who don't know much about the family soul, like myself at the time.

I had trouble sleeping the next nights. I could not think of anything else for a week. I didn't eat well either. It was nearly the same sensation I had when I first learned about the chakras, except the chakra knowledge was joyous—I'd felt excited and happy; but with this knowledge, I felt like I had gone through a meat grinder.

This family constellation knowledge was disturbing, but I knew in my heart that it was very real, and that both this new system and the chakras had a powerful role to play in my life.

To me, this was serious knowledge about the meaning of life, and it felt like part of the essence of the human condition. I was hooked and knew I had to research more, and that now I needed guidance from a live person.

I decided to call the facilitator who had given my friend a constellation session for her two-year-old daughter. I spoke to her on the phone for an hour. She was very kind and patient with me. I hesitantly booked an individual session. As soon as I booked the session, I could not sleep well for a week. I was so nervous that the day before the session, I called her up and canceled.

I remember giving the facilitator, and myself, a million excuses for postponing the session. The truth was, I was too scared to see the unknown contents of my "family field." I postponed having a session with her three times and focused on writing my thesis. I buried myself in the history of European and Native American social values and administrative organizations in South America and tried to forget about family constellations.

I knew the experience would be life changing and I could not handle going through emotional shifts as I was applying for a permanent position as a professor at the University of Brasilia. I told myself that, professionally, I could not lose my focus on that one.

Gratefully, I passed the exams and became a professor. I had about one hundred students to deal with, but now that I had gone through that rite of passage, I felt it was safe to go back to reading about constellations, and I polished the last details of my thesis. I felt the Native American cultures of *Tahuantinsuyu* and the *Tupinambás* in

Brazil had a strong connection with what Hellinger was saying about the soul in his family constellation theories.

When I finished and presented my PhD thesis to the board at the University of Brasilia, I felt such a release that in the same week I booked a session with the constellation facilitator whom I had spoken with on the phone a year before. This time I didn't cancel, and on that same week I was at her office.

I attended the individual session and was so impressed with what came up that in the same weekend I showed up in the group constellation she was organizing. As it turned out, she was just starting her one-year constellation training the next weekend. It felt like things were happening in synchronicity again, and since I didn't have the thesis or the professor exam to think about anymore, I had all the energy in the world to start this new training.

This was a one-year training with two hundred hours of theory and as many hours of practice as we were willing to give. My teacher and facilitator held three-hour constellation processes on Saturdays, with three constellations each, so we could spend about nine hours per week in group constellation practices if we wanted to. For two years I attended more than three hundred constellations easy, because I was there practically every Saturday, and on weeknights when she held them too.

My instructor certified constellation practitioners in a perspective she cocreated with another professor from the University of Brasilia, who specialized in archetypal images. In the beginning, I was not focused on becoming a therapist, but as a researcher I was fascinated to learn more about the theory and fundamental principles behind family constellations with hands-on practice sessions, and in combination with archetypal images, I was truly in heaven.

At the time, I knew the family constellations philosophy could contribute to my academic research about human nature, consciousness, and moral values. It was a new multidisciplinary field to learn about, and I knew I could start building a bridge between these different areas of knowledge. Hellinger, the creator of family constellations, combined philosophy with multicultural perspectives about the soul and therapeutic modalities, which is exactly what I love and believe in, so I felt happy and fulfilled every time

I thought about that. In my conscious mind, I kept telling myself I was interested in the theoretical basis of family constellations, which was why I wanted to explore it fully. The philosophy behind the modality is fascinating, very structured, and very solid.

I was satiating my intellectual interest with this new literature, but at the same time, while my conscious mind was busy with analytical thinking, a lot of soul healing and life connection was happening beyond what my conscious mind could fathom.

Things were happening in a much deeper and expanded level. From the moment I signed up for the one-year course, fast shifts were strangely happening to me in other areas of my life—almost like I had taken too long to be there and needed to catch up: Shifts such as leading a group of students in Native American researches in the political theory and moral philosophy perspective, which was a dream come true to me. Things such as getting an apartment exactly where I wanted to live, right in front of the water wells park. Things such as ending a painful long-distance relationship that was lagging along in years of heartbreak and meeting my husband a month later.

In the deeper and more dynamic levels of my consciousness, it felt like my Higher Self was gently guiding me to a major spiritual experience, and not just another layer of intellectual interest. What was going on was far beyond philosophical and intellectual knowledge, and it was not only deep, raw emotional work, but also exponential expansion of consciousness and alignment with an orderly, benign flow of life that connected me with the best energies life can offer.

It became clear to me that when we work on ourselves to get rid of emotional wounds and stop wasting our energy with painful memories, our awareness of self, personal growth, and spiritual connections kick in, and abundant, joyful things tend to happen very fast.

Throughout the constellation certification course, I had many insights. The strongest and most important one was that I especially felt an urge to bring crystals and stones to the classes. Secondly, I started to create and draw some very colorful images of nature I called "healing portals," and I felt I needed to give them to the people in the class.

As we learned the constellation principles and techniques, I was always giving people stones to hold during the constellation training and giving them colorful drawings as gifts I had personally made to hang on their walls for soul healing. I almost felt like a child doing this, but I did it anyway, because I began to understand I was healing my artistic wounds and weaving my passions together—human nature knowledge, nature, art, and spirituality. The people in class were very loving about it too. It was all very interesting and unpredictable.

I did feel strongly that a lot of the healing that was going on in my life was amplified or anchored by the presence of crystals and these images I created in the classes. And when I was taking the fifth module, right in the middle of the ten-module course, **The Cardinal Method of Life Connection** began to take shape in my mind.

Aside from the cultural values and organizational structures of the Native American societies I had been studying in South, Central, and North America, I was also interested in their spiritual wisdom.

Many of these cultures are very precise about the cardinal points as symbolic references to a spiritual life, and they teach us how to connect with the best life path, how to respect silence, and how to live from the heart (Castañeda, 1987).

Precise cardinal directions guide our life paths in the perspective of some of these traditional cultures. A few of them, like the Incas and Mayas, had geometrical and astrological references to these spiritual life paths. In my family constellations training, I began to observe some common truths between these cultures and constellation theory, and to connect the dots about how our present-day individual life paths can have similar soul challenges such as the ones described by ancient wisdoms.

I also began to observe the idea of belonging to family souls, cultural souls, and other group souls. Family constellations are all about knowing our place and our size in the family systems. Our rightful place and size in our families matters a lot to the archaic consciousness of the soul.

If we stand where we truly belong and acknowledge the place of all family members, we feel more confident about who we are and the best of life begins to flow. It can be literally considered a proportional geometric space. When we live from that space, our life path becomes meaningful and easy. We begin to make better choices about whom to connect with, what are the best decisions to make, and which are the best paths to follow.

Since in the constellations certification course we were simultaneously working with archetypal images, a lot of the Native American symbols I happened to be studying for my academic researches and the chakra images I had become familiar with since my teenage days started to make a specific kind of sense in my mind, as they were "layered" upon family constellation knowledge. At the time, I started calling this structure the Anahata Method (*Anahata* is the heart chakra), because all subtle energies converge to the heart, but I knew it was a temporary name.

Different knowledge from various parts of the world started clicking together in my head and creating a structure. As a researcher, I knew I needed to share this with other people to verify if it made sense. I asked my two instructors if I could present the blueprint of the multidisciplinary system that was developing in my head to them. They said yes.

The three of us met for two hours, and I explained my ideas and the logic behind them, using a multidisciplinary approach that combined aspects of Native American wisdoms; the Hindu chakras system; the ideas of an inner child, an ego, a real self, and a Higher Self; and the family constellation perspective.

It felt almost like submitting another thesis to a board, as they were deeply evaluating me and how this new system I was developing could also be a mirror image of my own psyche. The structure of what would later be called **The Cardinal Method of Life Connection (CMLC)** was already complex enough and felt so clear, both to me and to my instructors.

They both said it was consistent and were kind and supportive. They told me to observe myself and my life in each aspect of the **CMLC** as I thought about the structure I was unfolding. They told me we create mirror images of our inner world and manifest them in the outside world, and much of the information I was getting had to do with my own history. I told them I would pay attention to that, and they gave me permission to move forward and develop the work. We also agreed to present my ideas to the certification students at Vale da Lua, a beautiful place in nature where monthly constellations were held.

I was so overwhelmed with the **CMLC** that I asked if I could interrupt my constellation training and just participate in the constellation processes for a while. I needed to digest the whole thing, and I asked if I could continue with the certification modules in the following year. I told them that if I digested the information and structured the method as it was at the time, I would feel more secure about it. If I joined their class in the following year to finish the last modules, I would be able to read more, research more, and study more, and I could not do it going through so many of my own raw emotional healings in our training every month. I knew I could not do that and be a full-time professor at the university at the same time.

They said yes, because in their understanding every soul has a different rhythm and a different pace, which I was grateful for. I took some time off the training and kept attending all the constellations my instructor held on Saturdays, and some evenings in between, as I developed the structure of the method and got it all on paper as I organized my ideas. The following year, when I felt I was ready to finish the theoretical modules, I rejoined the class.

I finished the theoretical modules and got certified. **The Cardinal Method of Life Connection** as it is now clicked into place very quickly in my head after that, and I knew I had a system that connected four fundamental pillars of wisdoms to share with the world.

I needed to become more connected to my real self, and I knew being a professor was part of it but not the gravitational center of my being. Creating a life connection system in my journey involved all the aspects of the roads I had traveled, and since my academic background is on comparative theory and multidisciplinary systems, with the **CMLC** I have built bridges between different knowledge systems and connected them with the power of crystals. In this process, a lot of creative unfamiliar information that is exclusive to the **CMLC** emerged, and its uniqueness may be a contribution to life too.

When the theoretical blueprint was completely in place, I felt it was time to start practicing **The Cardinal Method of Life Connection** with the people I knew. I started to sketch out this book in 2011 and got volunteer friends to test the sessions for two years before I moved to the United States. Most of them were from my constellation course, and these people were extremely helpful in the first stages of the practical sessions with their suggestions and feedback.

I am truly grateful to all my friends and family in Brazil who have helped me and believed in the **CMLC,** by allowing me to see their personal journeys through this system. I thank them all with all my heart.

The Structure of The Cardinal Method of Life Connection
The **CMLC** is a consciousness-alignment system that uses crystals to provide progressive life connection and personal fulfillment to those who are willing to expand their consciousness and heal their souls. The gravitational center of the **CMLC** is the use of crystals to achieve these progressive levels of consciousness expansion, which consequently leads soul healing.

As inspirational references to achieve this state of being, the **CMLC** uses four fundamental pillars of knowledge: family constellations, Native American wisdoms, the Hindu chakras system, and contemporary concepts of the psyche, especially the ideas of an inner child, an ego, a real self, and a Higher Self.

The tools we use in the **CMLC** are the crystals, affirmations, conscious silence, and sea salt:

- Crystals and affirmations are the active energy of the **CMLC**. They encourage and allow the truth to surface and govern our lives.

- Conscious silence is the yin, the restful energy of awareness in the **CMLC**. It allows us to digest the process and encourages us to hold our peace with reality as it is.
- Sea salt brings the neutral energy of the **CMLC**, eliminating distortions, neutralizing past pain, and bringing us back to our natural state of the present moment in health and bliss.

The **CMLC** needs this natural state of being as a path to consciousness expansion, well-being, a clear mind for decision making, healthy emotions, and focus.

Connection with nature is also one of the fundamental energies of the **CMLC**. Many moral philosophers, both in the Eastern and Western worlds, have stated that the closer we are to nature, the healthier and happier we are as human beings (Locke, 2016; Rousseau, 2016; Thoreau, 2012; Patanjali, Carlos Eduardo Barbosa, 1999). The more we distance ourselves from nature, the more distorted our emotions and minds become, and we get more disconnected from our natural essences.

In a **CMLC** perspective, the key to a good and balanced life is not to live in isolation in a natural or wild environment. It simply involves constant contact with nature and the natural world, to make time to be in nature constantly and to simultaneously live in a healthy social world as well. Both nature and society are equally important in a **CMLC** perspective. Both types of relationships promote strong and healthy life connections we all need as human beings. When we lose life connection and self-connection, life is meaningless; we become unhappy, and eventually, unhealthy.

As a comparative systems researcher, I have woven together various principles of human nature and combined them with natural tools, such as affirmations, crystals, and salt, to create the **CMLC**. The four fundamental pillars of inspiration of the **CMLC** regarding human nature, for instance, all relate to crystals and are all discharged with salt. We use crystals in **CMLC** family constellations, and combine them with Native American wisdoms, the Hindu chakras system, and the dialectic movement of the inner child, the ego, and the real self in our psyches. We use crystals to connect to our Higher Selves as well.

In a **CMLC** session or practice, however, we are not really healing anything—we are aligning ourselves with our natural state of being and reestablishing a life connection. A life connection is a reactivation of natural circuits of consciousness and awareness in the energetic blueprints and geometries of our lives and our bodies, and we use crystals and other natural tools to reestablish this life connection.

To establish a life connection is to live from the essence of our beings and our natural selves. The focus of the **CMLC** is to establish a life connection that contributes to consciousness expansion and heals the soul by bringing forward the essence of our true being, and this happens, among other things, through your constant contact with nature. Nature manifests itself in our physical bodies and in crystals, plants, animals, and any living being. **The Cardinal Method of Life Connection** uses all these references as life connection tools.

The **CMLC** uses crystals in association with family constellation principles to align the soul (both individual and collective, which include our families and cultures of origin). Crystals are combined with Native American wisdoms to align us with the external world (which includes the physical, geographic, and social world we are immersed in). In association with the Hindu chakras system, we use crystals to align the individual self with the perfect energetic blueprints of our physical and subtle bodies.

Since the alignment of our consciousness with crystals eliminates distortions, or "spiritual errors" (Wood, 2004), the **CMLC** uses them to organize aspects of the psyche too. With practices and techniques, we progressively become a mirror image of our Higher Selves, feel everything in life more vividly, and think with a Higher Consciousness.

By studying therapeutic modalities and understanding the theory behind them, **The Cardinal Method of Life Connection** promotes connection with nature and a synthesis of the four systems of consciousness described above.

Living from the essence of our being means our lives will not be guided by the fragmented aspects of the psyche, such as painful memories of the soul, the wounded self-centeredness of the inner child, or the controlling arrogance of the ego. It will be guided from the perspective of our essences, our true nature, our real self, and the connection with the Higher Self.

Meditation, deep-breathing cycles, and contact with nature are great ways to establish a life connection. The more we practice with **CMLC** crystals, the more we will get insights in how to develop a lifestyle that includes these principles in our lives.

The practice of **The Cardinal Method of Life Connection** as a modality that uses crystals to bring life to its best alignments brings many shifts and substantial change. I have witnessed peoples' consciousness levels and lives shifting dramatically. When we have an open mind, awareness increases, and our life path becomes brighter because of the deep processes of consciousness expansion **CMLC** crystals and practices bring. We start to overcome limiting beliefs, abandon toxic relationships, move away from unhappy environments, and release emotional pain, and so many other aspects of our lives become lighter as we start to expand our consciousness.

Since in a life-connection perspective, what doesn't serve us will naturally leave us, as soon as we let go of limitations and attachments to the past, different, bigger, and better things come into our lives.

We start to attract better experiences, people who are more attuned with our essences begin to resonate more frequently with us, and we progressively become more aware of who we truly are and more connected to what we want and what we love.

In a life-connection process, we organically nurture our lives in healthier ways. As you keep reading this book, you will feel how understanding and overcoming the limiting aspects of life bring more pleasure, joy, freedom, and love as natural states of being. This is really a description of a spiritual life and a spiritual path, which does not have to be religious. When I say that my spirit guided me as I researched family constellations and soul-healing modalities, I mean "spirit" in a life-connection perspective—something that keeps us connected to God and to life in a very natural way.

The idea of "spirit" in **The Cardinal Method of Life Connection** can walk hand in hand with both religious and nonreligious perspectives. It just means we are on track and aligned with our life purpose, being truly who we are, and constantly expressing our essences and truth. This is the path to life connection we embrace in the **CMLC**, knowing that all healing comes from honesty, from progressively living in the truth and from the truth (Marin, 2006).

This can also be described as authenticity—simply being and going beyond the mind, the ego, intellectual abilities, and emotions as well. It is living from deep love for self and others, connected to the creative source of life energy we have in our hearts. From this source of the real self, we experience love, happiness, health, well-being, and joy. **Cardinal Method of Life Connection** practices allow this relationship with the spirit to surface. It connects us to the inner source of life, and we will naturally express ourselves from that place.

Living from personal truth is a universal condition for a healthy humanity—we all have our own unique expression in the world, and when we manifest it, everyone benefits. That is what **The Cardinal Method of Life Connection** aligns us with.

An important thing to be very mindful of in a **CMLC** journey is that this process is for mature people only, as Judy Cannato would say (Cannato, 2010) It is for people who are willing to take personal responsibility for their journeys. Do not expect the theory in this book, the practices, or the sessions, to be a car wash. Things do not start happening because someone in the outside world will save us, or because life will magically change without our personal commitment and effort, or that things will get better if we do not take inspired action every day.

Another important thing to understand is that emotional collapses or any type of "failure" we go through are not permanent, and that they have a reason to happen. They show us we are not on the right path. That is the only reason negative things happen to us, and **CMLC** crystals align us with what gives us the consciousness to understand life as it is, and connects us to what serves and nurtures us best.

Every time we try to live by following other points of reference that are not our personal truth (which come either from the wounded soul or inner child, the controlling ego, the distorted emotions, or our defense mechanisms), life is being guided by external forces. We may be living from trauma, cultural obligations, family traditions, social pressure, and other people's priorities. This is not honest living.

We are happy when we live from the truth of our being, and every time we get disconnected from inner truth, an annoying or painful episode will soon arise. When we insist on the wrong track, specific things will happen that will make us be more mindful or probably even turn our lives upside down. Life is easier when we understand that any kind of pain—physical, mental, emotional, or spiritual—is always a messenger of consciousness that tells us something we are doing is not aligned with our truth.

The **CMLC** helps us see how and why we are off track.

In practical terms, systems like the **CMLC** show us where and when we are missing the target, but our ability to see clearly is often compromised. My personal experience with crystals and the **CMLC**, and with many other people I have observed in years of experience as a student and professional, is that there can be a lot of conscious and unconscious resistance to spiritual growth coming from the wounded inner child, the controlling ego, and the limitations of the conscious mind. The truth is that self-connection and knowledge of self are inherently simple, unless there is resistance coming from painful emotional memories and a rigid mind.

In my case, I did not deliberately decide to connect with who I really am. I was always an enthusiastic student of spiritual traditions, but I was less inclined to hands-on soul searching and spiritual practices, unless I was going through rough times. Life happened in such a way, however, that the process of life connection ran me over, despite the unconscious resistance and hesitations of my conscious mind. It was my mission and something I needed to do, regardless of my inner-child stubbornness and the intellectual arrogance of my ego.

Things came to a point in my life at which I could no longer justify my painful experiences by blaming others. Playing victim never works, and despite all the years of therapy, I still did a lot of that without realizing it. Until I started understanding energy modalities and a spiritual approach to life outside the scope of regular therapy, I kept blaming others and creating a sugarcoated image of myself that was nothing but an ego trip. I could no longer sustain that when I decided to embrace energy-healing modalities and realized our minds create every single episode that happens in our lives. We are creators of our experiences, and no one else is to blame for the negativity we attract.

I guess I only fully realized this when I came in touch with family constellations, because of its collective soul and systemic perspective. I found the missing link in the equation of my downfalls—individually and collectively, I needed to heal. We need to work on ourselves individually and understand the collective environments we are immersed in to release our lives from "systemic entanglements" (Hellinger, 2012), and to free ourselves from the distortions of our own inner world as we create our realities.

General Overview of The Cardinal Method of Life Connection
Based in many traditional cultures, **The Cardinal Method of Life Connection** is specifically structured in the Zulu wisdom present in family constellations, Native American wisdoms about the truth and the power of crystals, and Hindu knowledge about chakras as centers of modification of consciousness—from limited to higher. A more contemporary view of human nature and human consciousness is also present in the **CMLC** as a fourth pillar, which relates to the inner child, the ego, the real self, and the Higher Self.

The structure of **The Cardinal Method of Life Connection** is based on these four fundamental pillars. Several other inspirations from Western and Eastern philosophy and other traditional societies are less evident, such as modern moral philosophy, ancient Greek archetypes, and the Enneagram, which are also important and incorporated in its theoretical design and practice.

With all these influences in mind, it is important to know that **The Cardinal Method of Life Connection** has a specific way to organize our understanding of human nature, consciousness, and the human experience on a theoretical level. It is also very simple and

THE CARDINAL METHOD OF LIFE CONNECTION

down to earth on a practical level. It is designed to help us find the path to healing by relying on our own abilities to see the truth of our lives—and **CMLC** crystals are here to help in this process.

When we are healing our souls, our true authentic selves naturally emerge—the spark of life or inner wisdom that lives inside us will start to rule our lives and guide us on our paths. This connection engages all of us in a benign flow of life and love, bringing beneficial connections and relationships that lead to fruitful, meaningful, fulfilling experiences.

CMLC distance and present sessions are always done with crystals. In **CMLC** practices, our emotional field is visualized, and issues are expressed to understand how aligned or not we are with our families of origin, especially our relationship with our mother and our father.

As we get more familiar with sessions, depending on how emotionally willing we are and how we respond to the initial shifts, the symbol of the arrow (which will be explained in chapter 4 of this book) may be used to observe our life purpose and how aligned or not we are with it.

In this stage, the perspective of life directions and elements of Native American wisdoms may come up to help cleanse emotions and traumas of family members and ancestors down to the seventh previous generation. Depending on the degree of commitment with our own healing, this session allows us to clearly visualize our spiritual mission in this lifetime.

On this second step, we connect to the outside world and nature. The inspiration for this in the **CMLC** comes especially from Native American wisdoms, though many traditional cultures in general may inspire us to do the same. Silent connection to nature is a crucial part of a self-connection and a life-connection journey, and we will experience the loving abundance of joy and peace when we read the information contained in chapter 4 of this book.

When we reach this "Arrow" stage, the first two major steps of **The Cardinal Method of Life Connection** have been taken. It is important to note that many people do not feel the need to keep going right away and may stay for many sessions in the first stage, visualizing the soul, before we reach the Arrow session.

Consciousness expansion and purification of emotional elements is never a linear process, and by no means should we pressure ourselves. The stage of focusing on our parents before moving forward to observe our ancestral lineages may often be enough for a long time, and we may wish to wait a little before we continue to the next stages of individual knowledge of self.

Focus on clearing immediate family issues, and finding the exact place where we belong to claim the strength that allows the abundance of a fulfilling life to flow, is a prerequisite for joy, love, well-being, and peace of mind—if we want to have an abundant human experience.

In the third step, the principles of **The Cardinal Method of Life Connection** are applied to a more subtle and individual level of free will and taking responsibility for self. This third step is described in chapter 5 of this book, and deals mostly with understanding of self, the tempting power of comfort zones we tend to adapt to, and clearing the blocked areas of our bodies and minds on chakra level. Each chakra expresses specific types of consciousness and carries very unique deviations from our virtuous core. When we understand the type of deviation each chakra brings, we become more conscious and potentially more responsible for our thoughts and actions.

This third stage of the **CMLC** focuses on your individual consciousness of emotions and attitudes by observing images of the Hindu chakra system and placing crystals on corresponding emotional and physical aspects that the chakras represent.

Our individual traumas, feelings, emotions, attitudes, decisions, and life experiences may often hold us back from consciousness expansion, because it takes effort and courage to clear them out. And again, by no means should we force ourselves to move forward when we do not have the will or the strength to do so yet. When the time is right, we will naturally feel an urge and a compelling movement to go for it.

In the chakras stage, sessions focus on the purification of feelings and emotions regarding the third generation (grandparents), second generation (parents), and ourselves. Concerning how these feelings and emotions affect our lives, we will always need to remind ourselves that no one is "haunted" by ancestors.

They are not "out to get us" in a family constellation and in a **CMLC** understanding. On the contrary. According to Bert Hellinger, it is the immature love of the child within us that unconsciously accesses painful stories in the family and clings to ancestors and their long-gone experiences. The immature love of the inner child creates fantasies to save them from pain or stands in shock with hidden issues and dreadful life experiences.

In family constellation and **Cardinal Method of Life Connection** sessions, we can see how people unconsciously choose to be focused on and entangled with ancestral painful experiences. The inner child will "magically" try to save them by repeating their stories in their own lives, trying to have a different outcome. But we can never change what has happened, and a lot of our energy is wasted in this sort of unconscious identification.

In this third stage of the **CMLC** journey, we visualize the family system as a layer upon the chakra system, and by representing the individual's own experience with crystals, we can understand the specific energy that is entangled in each chakra.

Usually, when we get to the third stage, we will likely be interested in the fourth and last stage of **The Cardinal Method of Life Connection**, which is individually the most challenging one, explained in chapter 6 of this book. In this layer of consciousness, we see ourselves as independent individuals, by ourselves, responsible for ourselves, with no one there to save us. By facing our own emotions, feelings, and attitudes for which we are responsible, we understand what has been crystalized in our childhood and unconsciously determining experiences in our adulthood without our awareness. The crystals will bring that information in the session very precisely.

It is not easy to admit that we are unconsciously choosing a specific painful path led by unprocessed and unrecognized emotions. And admitting we are responsible for absolutely everything that happens in our lives in a huge step in moving the path of a self-connection process and a life-connection journey.

In this fourth stage, we especially look at childhood promises and try to transmute them with contemporary notions of spirituality such as Higher Self, the inner child, the ego, and the real self. When we see the unconscious childhood promises that become self-fulfilling prophecies, promises we have made in childhood that damage our present adult lives by attracting and allowing negative experiences to happen, we begin to free our lives from self-sabotage and become more connected to love, life, health, and well-being.

These unconscious energies that block our life flow also relate to individual and collective karma, but mostly from our arrogance.

We become self-destructive to hurt others—to hurt those we love the most and who love us most, especially our parents. All the negativity unfolds into yet another layer of destructive energy, which is shame and guilt.

One of the major outcomes of a **CMLC** journey is, therefore, to release individual and collective self-destructive energies and guilt. Knowing that it can all be transmuted with alignment, personal effort, expansion of consciousness, and taking inspired action, things can change dramatically and become much brighter.

Painful memories and destructive behaviors we inherit from the past, unconsciously shared by the family soul and by the belief systems of our cultural backgrounds, influence our psyches more than we realize. When we understand that when life is not going so well because we may be unconsciously entangled in distortions, and that the choices we are making are not coming from the heart, but from our loyalty to past pain, shifts can happen very quickly.

Dialectic Movements in the CMLC
A dialectic movement can be described as the flow of energy between a thesis, an antithesis, and a synthesis (Hegel, 1977).

The thesis is the first given factor to be observed, which will be shifted after an interaction with its antithesis, which is its complete opposite. For instance, when a white color is contrasted with a black color, the white color is the thesis and the black color is the antithesis.

A synthesis is when opposites interact and are mixed together to create a third reality or result that integrates, overcomes, and surpasses the thesis and the antithesis. The result of this interaction will be a synthesis of "gray," which includes both colors, or opposites, and surpasses them, going a step further in experience and strength.

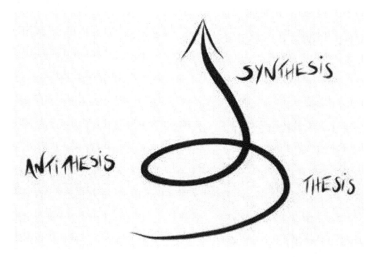

In a **CMLC** perspective, a child is a synthesis of a father (synthesis) and mother (antithesis). The child is a result of the interaction between mother and father. When this child grows up and becomes a new thesis, finds a partner (an antithesis), and together they have a child, they create a synthesis which is also a new thesis. The movement of energy is dialectic: all beings find antithesis and create new synthesis in the world all the time. This is a simple description of dialectic interaction.

Our human experience can be observed as a constant dialectic movement in which we come into the world and interact with different realities, and because of that interaction, our minds become broader and unfold themselves in a synthesis of expansion, by incorporating that new experience.

In the **CMLC**, there is a permanent dialectic movement in the interaction between the person, the crystals, and the consciousness outcome that results from this interaction. This dialectic movement is simple and profound. A person will come with his or her issues and distortions that are present in his or her energetic field. The crystals' internal geometry, which has a higher vibration compared to the distortions of our conscious and unconscious minds, will "remind" our energetic field of a healthier, more benign state of being, realigning our minds and energetic frequencies with this higher and natural vibration.

CMLC dialectic movements simply mean that there are always three forces at play: the individual's internal world, crystals, and the expanded consciousness that results from this interaction.

Synthesizing CMLC Information
The most important thing to understand is that all these inspirational references converge in one principle that is the core of **The Cardinal Method of Life Connection**: connecting to truth, expanding consciousness, and creating a benign flow of energy. This result is an abundant flow, a synthesis, between our real selves and life.

The best of life happens when we create our journey from an abundant perspective and from the inspired actions of the real self, and not from the wounded soul, the ego, the inner child, or any other destructive unconscious force within our psyches. When the real self is strong and guides our lives, everything flows and clicks into place, and we begin to expand our minds as we start living from the inspiration of the Higher Self through a connection with the real self and higher-consciousness experiences.

In a **CMLC** perspective, the physical world can be constantly or even permanently connected to the spiritual world, inspired by a life connection with God—or not. When there is no connection between physical matter and Higher Consciousness, that separation creates a dualistic mind, which is one of the things we can overcome with **CMLC** experiences. When we create synthesis with crystal alignments and the guidance of the Higher Self, it helps us understand that the material world and the spiritual world are not separate, but one.

The more we engage in life-connection experiences, the more we disengage from the dualistic mind and come back to unity. When material manifestations and our unique spiritual realities, or authentic self-expression, become one, life flows. The problem is when our material realities manifest distortions. *When there is a life connection,* and there are no, or few, distorted interferences that separate manifestation from true, pure essence, we can literally feel heaven on Earth.

After many years of studying and writing, I have finally described the fundamental pillars of **The Cardinal Method of Life Connection** here in this book. I hope it contributes to the expansion of consciousness of all readers, and especially that it helps those who are willing to open their hearts and lives to the free flow of endless, loving, healthy joy and abundance we are all here to enjoy on this planet.

With this in our hearts and minds, let's start the journey now.

1

UNDERSTANDING HIGHER CONSCIOUSNESS

The **CMLC** considers that there are three levels of consciousness human beings can develop: **functional**, **individual,** and **Higher**. Crystals help us take the steps into the expansion of these levels, aligning our awareness and inner worlds with progressively higher vibrations.

The first level of consciousness in a **CMLC** perspective is **functional consciousness**, which is a logical, natural energetic blueprint we follow in "autopilot mode." Functional consciousness is almost instinctive. It expresses itself in our lives as we behave and think as a biological human species. On the soul level, it expresses itself through the moral values of our families and cultures.

Functional consciousness is preestablished and automatic, and it is predominant on the three lower chakras of the body. In this level, we behave as an expression of a collective existence, dormant to our individuality and to individual creativity. We reproduce an energetic blueprint of conservation and continuity. This functional level is benign and balanced in nature. All interactions, including conflicts, are necessary and have a purpose, but we are not aware of our individuality—we just express our instincts and social needs automatically.

The second level of consciousness is the **individual level**. On this level, we are aware of ourselves as human beings, and as a unique manifestation of the human species. Self-awareness begins on the solar plexus, where it coexists with functional consciousness and is predominant on the level of the heart and throat chakras. In individual consciousness, we affirm and assert ourselves, we may create conflict when we feel we are being abused or invaded, and we see and respect the individuality of others.

Self-awareness is a necessary step in the expansion of consciousness, but its purpose is to overcome itself in the next step, which is the third level of Higher, universal, or cosmic consciousness. **Higher Consciousness** means we are transcending reactions of individual consciousness and seeing ourselves as part of a bigger picture without feeling separate from it. This level is predominant on the third-eye and crown chakras, where we develop a sense of belonging to a cosmic, infinite reality, immersing ourselves in consciousness as it is, and understanding consciousness as all there is. We predominantly observe on this level, where everything happens in awareness, silence, and awe. We contemplate life in amazement, connect to it, allow its flow in our being, and preserve its benign energy.

When we start living from a Higher Consciousness perspective, the information that surfaces with **CMLC** practices releases many of our limitations. For those who are willing to take responsibility for life and self, commit to change, sustain a new lifestyle and healthier ways of thinking, it works beyond our expectations.

The **CMLC** also helps to understand how individual experiences relate to our inner world, as unfolding layers of our own consciousness. We understand how we create our experiences in the outside world and free ourselves from victim mode. In this perspective, whether we like it or not, any experience we go through is a conscious or unconscious mirror image of what is inside us—in our minds, souls, hearts, and being.

Since some aspects of our psyches are individual, and others are collective, the **CMLC** literally gives us an overview of a 360-degree panorama of our human experience. Our family, cultures, and external world are shared experiences and have a collective nature. The chakras system, the Higher self, the inner child, and the ego are some of our individual aspects.

Three important principles guide the **CMLC**. The first is that all life connection comes from living and being in the truth, and this requires clarity of mind. We need to be clear about our life experiences, about what we want for our lives, and about what we love and what makes us happy. If we dedicate some time to make an honest list about the truth of who we are, what we want, and what our happiness goals are, we begin to get clear about what it takes to achieve these goals—and if we are willing to take the steps.

The second important principle about the **CMLC** is to commit to an allowing attitude, especially allowing the free flow of love into our lives. And love in this sense means a mature love that respects healthy boundaries and is not clingy and dependent. Many people have a very intense or suffocating idea of love and may be living in symbiotic, infantile relationships that come hand in hand with attachment, instead of allowing a free flow of joyful love to enter their lives.

It is important to discern these two kinds of love: the symbiotic and immature type, and the abundant and free type, which understands boundaries and comes with creative spurs and constant expansion. The free flow of mature love always comes with abundance. Any scarcity or conditional understandings may be coming from other sources of energy that are camouflaged as love, such as neediness, attachment, childhood wounds, and manipulation. It is important to be at least willing to discern between the two to engage in a **CMLC** journey.

What we call a free flow of mature love is a balance between love and freedom. Another obstacle to the free flow of love is that many people are conditioned to resist it, even if consciously this is theoretically what we all want as adult human beings. Allowing the free flow of love to enter our lives is relatively simple if we just be ourselves and live from the truth. However, our internal worlds tend to resist the best of life because of unconscious suffering, the habit to cultivate emotional pain, loyalty to the suffering of loved ones, and fear of change. These obstacles exist both in the conscious and the unconscious mind.

Our conscious and unconscious limiting beliefs are very strong, and so is the lack of self-love most of us tend to experience. Observe yourself from your heart and see if, and when, you are setting yourself up to resist the free flow of love in our lives. Loyalty to the suffering others can be suffocating, especially our parents, siblings, and ancestors.

For instance, if parents and ancestors had unhappy lives, we may feel guilty about leading a happy and fulfilled life. Other obstacles can also come from cultural traces, and each culture has different limitations. If we commit to look inside with clarity and develop not only self-love and a clear mind, but also conscious, healthy boundaries, this can all be balanced, and we can be aligned with the free flow of love and the best of life.

The third important thing about the **CMLC** is that when we talk about "the soul" in a **Cardinal Method of Life Connection** perspective, it has a double nature of being both collective and individual, and a spiritual connotation that is not a mystic one. The soul is part of our psyches and a natural part of the human condition, very much like our minds, feelings, and physical bodies.

In a **CMLC** perspective, the soul and the spirit are natural aspects of us, and not supernatural concepts. They do have an immaterial nature, and the reality of the soul and spirit can be understood by our mental and by our emotional faculties. It is a universal, very real part of who we are as human beings, and not as supernatural and transcendent as we tend to think—if we stop living exclusively from the limitations of our conscious minds and start living from the perspective of Higher Consciousness and the Higher Self.

The purpose of **The Cardinal Method of Life Connection** is to help align our whole being with Higher Consciousness levels through the use of crystals, and promote consciousness expansion. In this path, we connect to an abundant life of freedom, love, and joy. When alignment with this abundant flow of life begins, we witness the alignment of imbalances in all areas of life. Excessive fear, uncontrolled anger, emotional attachments, and feelings of anxiety will also be released. As we start living in more connection with the truth, our life quality increases immensely.

Truth, Love, and Joy
Truth, love, and joy are natural states of being and part of functional consciousness. When these three energies are blocked or distorted, life does not flow as strongly as it should. When we align with truth, love, and joy, we can connect to other levels of consciousness expansion, such as freedom and Higher Consciousness.

We tend to be very comfortable with love and joy, but sometimes the truth is not very easy to face and makes us uncomfortable. In a **CMLC** perspective, the truth is threefold, meaning it comes with healing energy and protection of our physical and moral integrity as well. This means the truth heals, and since all healing comes from honesty (Marin, 2006), when we live in the truth we are naturally protected from any kind of harm. Many people feel guilty about admitting the truth to themselves and to others. However, as Giles Marin said, all healing comes from honesty, and if we want to lead a good, healthy, fulfilled life, we cannot live in illusions, lies, distortions, or denial.

In a **CMLC** perspective, there are two distorted relationships with the truth we need to overcome. One is avoiding the truth, and the other is feeling guilty about it. We avoid the truth because it is sometimes painful to us and or to others. When we avoid the truth, it shows up in our lives through subtle languages of consciousness, such as dreams, signs, or insights in meditation. When we don't dream or pay attention to subtle signs, and when we do not meditate, consciousness speaks to us in more aggressive ways, such as unhappy episodes, open conflict, accidents, and diseases.

To face the truth, we must honestly observe which areas of our lives are unpleasant or could be better. Then we ask ourselves why things are not flowing so well, and most importantly, what can we do about it to make it better. There is always a solution, but when we do not have the courage to change, we disconnect from the truth and begin to live an unauthentic life, where there is no mature love and rarely abundant joy.

The Cardinal Method of Life Connection considers love and abundance to be general attributes of life. Love is our natural state of being, as is joy. The purpose of life is to express our love in the world and develop personal power and wisdom, which we are necessarily born with. Love is natural and automatic, but personal power and wisdom are not. We learn them in our journey and they coexist with love and joy if we remain connected to our path.

Our natural states of love and joy get corrupted and distorted by traumatic life experiences and inherited trauma. To remain connected to love and joy and to develop our personal power and wisdom, we must clear away trauma and distortions from our minds, our bodies, and our hearts. These distortions are present in our inner worlds because of past life experiences and active pain from ancestors.

Connection with crystals reminds us of our natural state of love and joy and clear the way to develop our talents and wisdom. When we are in a clear state, we connect to the general loving abundance of life and the world, and others. To connect to others in a joyful, loving way is part of a moral understanding of the world, which is present in many spiritual and religious traditions, and in moral philosophy.

This loving, abundant, moral concept of life reconnects us to the natural world with a sense of connection and belonging. This is a free choice and should be observed as a moral perspective. Crystals and stones are present in our journey as consciousness reminders and companions on our paths, and that connection rarely happens in an obvious way.

It is part of natural living and deep awareness. When we are in this state, we do not control anything—we do our part and stay present in the moment. It is much better—and a lot more fun—to surrender to the divine mystery of life, in which crystals play a huge role.

The Renaissance and Modern Moral Philosophy
From a dualistic perspective, we feel like our lives consist of an individual, personal existence in a physical world, and that we are separate from that world, be it geographic or social. This concept of an independent, immediate experience of individuality in the world is the gravitational center of many modern and contemporary sociological and moral theories.

Many thinkers inspire the **CMLC** in its idea of the human experience, and Leonardo da Vinci is possibly the most important one. Da Vinci is an inspiration because he promoted a harmonious integration among nature, art, science, philosophy, and technology, and as a humanist, he also included a very human type of spirituality in his daily living (da Vinci, 2010). For the **CMLC**, he is especially important because of his passion for technology and his dedication to geometry and proportion.

The **CMLC** is a soul technology modality, and proportion is a key element to organize our inner world and our lives. Da Vinci spoke of proportion in the perfect form of physical matter and physical bodies, and in the **CMLC** the proportion of matter and energy in sessions is very important (for example, the size of the crystals we use).

On the emotionalplain, the **CMLC** takes the idea of proportion to another level of understanding, which is further explored in moral philosophy. When we act and react proportionally, we tend to avoid problems and develop an ability to keep both internal and external peace.

Regarding proportion and geometry, for the **CMLC** the soul is considered a geometric canvas or blueprint of energy. Inspired by some of da Vinci's concepts, and observing how his mind worked, the **CMLC** can be considered "technology" for the soul, since the ideas of geometry, precise movement, and proportion are fundamental for this system.

Moving forward in time, Thomas Hobbes, a very controversial moral philosopher and political theorist, observes art and science as human contributions to the world that are superior to nature. Hobbes's philosophy states that human reason can use what nature gives us and go beyond natural creations with art and science, upgrading our life quality on many levels. However, unlike da Vinci, Hobbes focused on the distortions and chaos created by what he considered to be the manifestations of human nature and saw human beings as naturally destructive.

To Hobbes, each individual human being is determined by his or her internal world of pure subjectivity. To him, each person has such a unique, complex, and vast internal world that it is impossible to draw a pattern of what makes each one of us happy. Hobbes also said that human nature is characterized by a self-centered, egotistic state of mind that leads to permanent separation, using the image of constant movement and collision of molecules in the Newtonian model. In his understanding, on a social level, because of such unique internal subjectivity, human beings inevitably tend to engage in conflict, ultimately leading collective social realities into physical war. He stated that the war of all against all is, before all else, a permanent spiritual war, in which all people are intrinsically competitive, affirming that "Man is the wolf of man" (Hobbes, 2010, 1994).

Because of his focus on conflict and the permanent danger of mutual destruction, Hobbes is a philosopher of fear. He describes human fear and the fight-or-flight mechanism in a very masterful way. The problem is that he considers fear, self-centeredness, and separation as the essence of human nature and our natural state of being. In a **CMLC** perspective, however, this is not what human nature is all about—it is a reaction to dangerous situations that perpetuates itself in many cultures and may become, or has become, a distorted and constant part of the human condition.

Aside from fear, our self-centered "inclinations" are described by Hobbes mainly as variations of laziness and of cupidity. To him, each internal world is a subjective mystery, but we are mainly moved by laziness and/or cupidity and tend to fear others as potential threats to our best individual, egotistic interests.

Hobbes is an important reference for the **CMLC** not only as an antagonist to the **CMLC** perspective, but because of his idea of human inclinations toward conflict, what he describes as human nature is, in a **CMLC** perspective, a description of human distortions that can be released with energy-healing sessions and consciousness expansion with crystals. They are a result of living from a dualistic perspective and not from the integration of all aspects of our psyches or from the truth of the heart. Hobbes's "state of nature" describes distortions that can be healed, or theses that find their antitheses in **CMLC** crystal energy and that may result in a synthesis of consciousness expansion.

On another note, Hobbes would say only the use of reason could contain our passions and destructive, self-absorbed ideas, feelings, and behaviors. In his perspective, by using logical thinking and objective reasoning, one can control primitive aspects of the inner world.

Hobbes did not speak of a Higher Consciousness, though, and explicitly disqualified faith and a spiritual life. In a **CMLC** perspective, reason is indeed a strong tool of the human mind, and it is fundamental to understand our overreactive behaviors. The use of reason is important, but is must be associated with and guided by higher wisdom and moral values, such as honest living and living from Dharma (Veltheim, 2003). As Dr. John Veltheim would say, reason and logical thinking are activities of the brain, and the brain is a processor of information with no creativity or wisdom of its own (Veltheim and Muiznieks, 2013).

Therefore, in a **CMLC** perspective, reason is necessary but not sufficient to be the ultimate decision maker in our lives. It should ideally serve more sophisticated aspects of the psyche, such as our real self and Higher Consciousness.

John Locke, on another level of observation, speaks of human nature as benign, peaceful, social, and cooperative. To him, the world is intrinsically a good, harmonious place, and people are naturally kind and social. However, in Locke's perspective, human nature is also weak and prone to fall into temptation. In his theory, we tend to give in to allurements and often make mistakes because of our weak nature. Influenced by Christian ideas in a religious perspective, Locke believes we fall too quickly into temptation and end up developing immediate reaction patterns and superficial desires (Locke, 2008, 2016).

The key to keep ourselves on track and to avoid "taking the baits" of temptation is to use reason and measure our actions and reactions. Like da Vinci, Locke also saw proportion as one of the keys to a balanced, healthy life, especially when we use reason to measure the proportion of our emotional reactions to whatever seems to damage what we care for. A way to keep our lives on track is to not overly react emotionally, and to be mindful of the proportion of our actions.

Another important philosopher for **The Cardinal Method of Life Connection** who encourages objective, logical thinking to balance distorted emotions is Immanuel Kant. He also spoke of a benign nature within us, which should always be cultivated. In Kant's moral philosophy, we are born with an internal moral compass, which he calls "the moral law within." This moral compass propels us forward into a good life path. When we connect to this benign core of the moral law within and live from a place of harmony, we live from the truth and are literally contributing to peace on the individual and the social level (Kant, 2016).

In the **CMLC** perspective, the nature of life is indeed benign, and reason is used to understand and balance emotions, but not to neutralize them. In the **CMLC**, reality is abundant and full of life, and we have access to all the goodness of the world if our real selves and Higher Selves are synchronized with the natural, benign flow of life. Our wounded inner child and controlling ego, however, go in the opposite direction of this benign current and block the flow of life.

Integration of Comparative Methodologies

The **CMLC** adopts a multidisciplinary perspective that combines aspects of different theories and bodies of knowledge. These theoretical elements are woven together in a specific way when observed as part of the **CMLC** in a new innovative structure.

Max Weber was an expert of comparative cultures and methodologies. When comparing "human rationality" and "reality," he affirmed that one was the opposite of the other. To him, rationality is by nature limited, finite, controlled, logical, systematic, orderly, and understandable to the human mind. Reality, on the other hand, is unlimited, infinite, chaotic, unfathomable, and inapprehensible by the human mind. There is an absolute polarized contrast between the nature of these two phenomena.

To Weber, the concept of rationality is different than the idea of reason—it is a human faculty that varies in each person, as a subjective mental processing mechanism. When we combine this understanding with Thomas Hobbes's perspective of human subjectivity, rationality in Weber's perspective can be observed as mental processes that constantly confirm and reaffirm our individual experiences. When we do that, we automatically assume that our subjective individual presumptions are "the objective truth," or we generalize our personal experience as such.

A Jungian or even a spiritual approach to life, however, will encourage us to understand that the outside world is much larger than we think or can even fathom, and that our individual experiences will create understandings or filters that distort our perception of the nature and dimension/proportion of things.

The experiences we attract into our lives will be created by these distorted filters, and the framework of the outside world we experience will be a mirror image of what happens in our psyches, but these experiences are only a very small fraction of reality, which is much broader and can be better, more benign, and more abundant than we think.

Carl Jung, several sources of Native American wisdoms, Buddhism, Vedanta, and many other schools of knowledge would agree to this assumption, which goes beyond our rationality and our distorted conclusions and mental filters. We are now encompassing an approach that includes reason and enters the realm of the unconscious mind.

Contemporary Thinkers of the Unconscious Mind
Sigmund Freud is the father of psychoanalysis, and he brought the idea that the unconscious mind is more powerful than the conscious mind into the world (Freud, 2016). The individual unconscious mind rules a lot of our behavior in his perspective.

If we expand Freud's approach and observe this from an energetic perspective, not only is the unconscious mind more powerful, but it also attracts and creates our life experiences with great power. The more we expand our Higher Consciousness, however, the less powerful the unconscious mind is. Its contents can be neutralized and will not be able to create our experiences anymore. Our lives will then be created from a much healthier, more benign space.

Carl Jung went beyond Freud in the idea of an unconscious mind because he said that not only do we have an individual unconscious mind, but are also constantly tapping into and being guided by what Jung called the "collective unconscious mind" (Jung C. G., 1981, 2010).

The collective unconscious expresses universal archetypes that all individuals in all cultures relate to on conscious or unconscious levels. The archetypes are titles and roles we live by, such as the mother, the father, the warrior, the healer, the artist, the fool, the lover, the wife, the husband, and so many others. The individual conscious and unconscious mind is immersed in the collective unconscious, and often guided by it without real awareness.

In this train of thought, Clarissa Pinkola Estés, author of the book *Women Who Run with the Wolves* (1997), speaks of how understanding the contents of our psyches promotes a strong life connection that gives our life journey meaning and purpose. This is a book about the female psyche, but a lot of what is said here is universal and can be applied to both women and men.

One important thing to align us with the truth of our beings is to learn about archetypes and to hear stories about the human soul in diverse cultural journeys. Stories and archetypes nurture the soul in Estés's perspective, and the **CMLC** is very aligned with this principle.

Since stories nurture and heal the soul because they connect us to the truth, in the **CMLC** practices it is always advisable to hold crystals as we read or hear powerful stories. They are truly life-changing healing tools, and the stories of our lives and our family history may shift to higher levels of consciousness when stories are told and crystals are present to help our minds align with the best flow of objective, clear information and release wounds and grudges.

The Role of CMLC Crystals with Higher Consciousness, the Conscious Mind, and the Unconscious Mind

The **CMLC** brings alignment of our lives with the real, true selves through the power of crystals. Native American wisdoms bring knowledge about the consciousness aspect of crystals. The Native American tradition affirms that crystals are very old beings and that they store all the information there is in the planet because they have been around for so long.

In the **CMLC** perspective, the relationship between crystals and how they help us tune in to accurate information is that their internal geometry has a higher vibration compared to the distortions of our subjectivity. When there is a dialectic interaction between a crystal's internal structure and human minds, our energetic field is aligned by the organized higher vibration of the crystal, and the result, or synthesis, is clarity of mind and access to or attunement to precise information. This connection encourages insights and expansion of consciousness.

In my opinion, crystals are unique consciousness tools that bring precise streams of information to our lives. This means they can act like stem cells that adapt themselves to specific issues and moments. They function in diverse ways in our lives according to the kind of issue we are dealing with, the kind of answers we need in each circumstance of life, and what is going on in the present moment.

Crystals will bring us flashes and insights that are very specific to our life experiences. Their attributes and information are not necessarily restricted to what is said in books or crystal blogs about the general nature of different crystals. There are, indeed, general attributes to each type of crystal, but each person may have a very specific and unique experience with the same crystal or crystal specimen in different moments. Someone else may hold the same crystal and have completely distinct experiences.

In my journey of twenty-five years working with crystals, what I can attest so far is that all crystals, as many Native American cultures acknowledge, allow the truth to surface, and with the truth, comes conscious awareness that heals the soul. With these insights, we do not need to attract any painful experiences to see the truth—we choose to connect to the truth and do something about whatever is causing us problems without suffering so much. In a way, it is preventive of painful experience and is a healing and a protective mechanism.

Together with the truth, I have also observed that crystals bring an energy of love and joy. In the **CMLC**, crystals have a threefold energy of truth (which includes healing and protection for Native Americans), love, and joy. The state of mind of living from the truth and creating love and joy connects us to the abundance of life.

As said before, in my experience crystals tend to act like "stem cells" and behave in unusual ways with different people. Yes, there are general attributes, and general healing properties, but specific information and insight moments shift and expand each person's consciousness in very particular ways. This means general attributes, such as self-love for rose quartz, or prosperity for citrines, depending on the circumstance, may come to us through other crystals even more intensely, because of our specific individual energy fields.

For example, if you need to strengthen the prosperity area of our lives, citrines will help you in a general sense, but other crystals that are more attuned to your specific energy may be even more powerful. If your professional strength is communication, aquamarine may help you even more in creating prosperity. If you tune in to your own energy or get information from energy experts that you trust, you may be surprised with the nonobvious nature of crystals, and maybe stones you'd never think of could work better as prosperity enhancers.

This means general knowledge from books is important, but we can always go beyond and sharpen our intuition with practice. We must always try to go beyond the obvious and feel our own energy with practices and energy attunements. The actual, complete crystal experience may not fit into the preset models found in books.

There is some consensus about the properties of many crystals, but there is a lot more to them than what books say. Personal experience will give us the most important and accurate information we can get. The most crucial thing about crystals, in my opinion, is our actual and practical relationship with each specimen we get in touch with.

Since in individual experiences, the alignment properties of crystals are usually not obvious, a considerable amount of research still needs to be done about that. There are general attributes, aspects, and truths about specific crystals, but crystals are intrinsically holographic and can act in many ways according to individual needs and circumstances.

In my research their uniqueness first relates to their geometrical internal structure, their specific hue and saturation of color, and how words and sounds reverberate within their internal structure. Secondly, we observe where they are placed in environments, or on the physical body as jewelry or therapeutic stones in energy healing sessions. Thirdly, we observe the way they are polished and shaped.

The essential point is that depending on the circumstances and the moment, the way stones act in our lives can change. Our conscious mind tends to be controlling, and we want to predict how crystals will always behave, thinking that will be exactly as the books say. Ironically, crystal behavior is not written in stone at all.

What we can be assured, though, is that they will always raise the vibration of the person or environment, they will always tend to allow the truth to surface if we have an allowing mind, and they will bring love and joy to our lives. Anything more specific than that will depend on the moment and the changing circumstances.

Our conscious mind always tries to understand and control everything, including information about crystals, but the truth is that most of life is unfathomable to the conscious mind (Veltheim, 2011). Crystals have a lot to help heal on the unconscious level—more than we can imagine—so it is better to ignore the conscious mind and let the crystals do the work. We can't possibly grasp their depth with the limits of our conscious minds that strictly follow books or our own assumptions.

It is also important to think of our relationship with crystals as horizontal. They are not in our service. Think of them as helpful tools that can help you a story, give you accurate information about your inner world, and encourage love and joy in your life. If we follow Native American wisdoms and engage in a state of mind in which there is no hierarchy or difference in consciousness of truth, healing, and protection between human beings, animals, plants, and crystals, we will be more successful.

This does not mean crystals and stones have individual consciousness and are self-aware, but that they align functional consciousness and our minds so we can develop and increase our self-awareness.

All crystals that touch our lives have a path, a role, and a mission with us. Your intuition will guide us in what to do with them, whom to give them to, and where to place them. Always remember that the flow of information and energy of the stones is very dynamic, and anyone who connects with a crystal is already healing and progressing energy in their journey to wholeness.

As I said before, in **The Cardinal Method of Life Connection** a lot of the healing and loving energy comes from crystals, and a lot of it also emanates from our virtuous core, or Higher Self, and our own ability of self-healing.

In the understanding of many Native American cultures (and other traditional cultures all over the world as well), *crystals connect us to the truth by revealing accurate information, and through accurate information they encourage expansion of consciousness.* When we are connected to the truth in a continuous flow of consciousness expansion, we attract meaningful, good experiences to our lives without effort.

The relationship between crystals and our own self-healing abilities is simple. The presence of crystals in **Cardinal Method of Life Connection** sessions and practices encourages and activates our own self-healing abilities, if we are willing to change our lives and change our thinking, as additional information and awareness become available. The awareness of the information can help repair virtually all areas of our lives that need alignment and integration—relationships, physical health, financial or professional issues, happiness, and joy.

In this flow of energy, **The Cardinal Method of Life Connection** uses crystals for healing and alignment of our lives to the best path you can follow—the path of your truth. As a process of knowing our true selves through this multidisciplinary approach, consistent contact with **Cardinal Method of Life Connection** crystals sharpens our intuition and helps our emotional healing processes.

Native American wisdoms (Sams, 1990) say that crystals allow accurate information to surface because, as very ancient beings of nature, they have a natural ability that encourages us to get in touch with the core of our being and our natural selves beyond the elaborations of the rational mind. When the awareness of our true selves surfaces in the presence of crystals, the insights we will get from them can potentially reveal the root cause of any given problem in a flash of inspiration or insight. The purpose of **The Cardinal Method of Life Connection** is that with the contact with crystals, we can heal emotional wounds and our relationships on all levels, enjoying life in its most wonderful potentials.

Crystal healing comes from being in touch with very concrete beings of nature and nature itself. Connecting to the natural world and with our own nature, it is easier to connect to the abundant love flow we are designed to experience. *Love is our natural state of being.* And crystals (plants and animals as well) bring us back to this natural state of being via a loving energy that heals and repairs the soul.

In a practical sense, crystals have a specific structure that allows healing to happen in a **Cardinal Method of Life Connection** context. The most important things to observe in this perspective of a healing system are

1. the internal geometry of crystals, which organize the energies of the soul and of our being;
2. the colors of the crystals and their specific hues and saturation;
3. the sounds we make in the presence of crystals, which can be prayers, mantras, sacred words, sacred names, and affirmations.

The shape of each crystal is important but secondary in a **Cardinal Method of Life Connection** perspective. The most important aspects are the internal geometry, the colors, and the hues or saturation of the specimen. It is the internal geometry and the color that mostly bring us back to the natural state of loving abundance and joy. This state allows us to live in the present moment, which is connected to the spiritual idea of a zero-point field.

Zero-Point Field
In a **CMLC** perspective, "zero-point field" is a symbolic reference to a state of stillness in which all painful memories from the past are neutralized. They will not be erased, but they will not trigger emotionally charged behavior, reactions, and projections anymore.

The internal geometry of crystals realigns our energy and brings us back to our natural state of love, health, and well-being. Clear quartz is the **CMLC** master stone to bring us back to a zero-point field, and it is up to us to sustain and maintain that state in our consciousness.

As Goethe would say,

> I have come to the conclusion that *I am the decisive element*. It is my personal approach that creates the climate. It is my daily mood that makes the weather. I possess tremendous power to make life miserable or joyous. I can be a tool of torture or an instrument of inspiration; I can humiliate or humor, hurt or heal. In all situations, it is my response that decides whether a crisis is escalated or de-escalated, and a person humanized or dehumanized If we treat people as they are, we make them worse. If we treat people as they ought to be, we can help them become what they can become. (adapted from a quote by Johann Wolfgang von Goethe, Goethe, 2012)

In the Ho'oponopono philosophy of life, a person can live from an intentional place of personal choices or surrender to a higher power (Vitale, J. and I. H. Len., 2008). This second option of life means living from zero-point field, through divine inspiration from the universe, in which there is true and absolute peace and there are no desires, because desires are no longer necessary—we already have all we need, and more. We do not have to think about our intentions because we are connected to an infinite source of abundance and become a vehicle of divine expression.

On the other hand, when we have desires or intentions, it is possible that our conscious minds may be trying to create our lives from our distortions (Vitale, 2013). In this perspective, if there is attachment to free will, there is a need for control over life and a false sense of omnipotence that stems from expectations. Expectations can frustrate us, and they ultimately lead to stress, doubt, agony, despair, and in extreme cases, even madness.

This understanding may be complementary to the idea of our inner child's arrogance and the immature love of the child described by Bert Hellinger and further discussed in chapter 3 of this book. If we are guided by emotions that give us an illusion of control, we may be living from a place where we unconsciously try to soften the suffering of our collective family soul. We may be living from programmed childhood fantasies that can last a lifetime.

The **CMLC** uses crystals to release this type of unconscious programming. If we have a receptive mind, **CMLC** crystals can help heal these emotional fantasies, releasing your blockages so life can follow its natural flow and you can fulfill our lives purpose.

Of all the crystals on this planet, clear quartz is the most efficient one to integrate our psyches and connect us to the benign energies of zero point. It is the most important crystal in **The Cardinal Method of Life Connection** both for individual and collective life-connection processes. Clear qartz will act as an eliminator of distortions in any situation; it is the most powerful "**CMLC** crystal stem cell" because in the **CMLC** it brings all energies back to zero point. When in doubt, we can use clear quartz in our **CMLC** practices, and we will never go wrong.

What Can Block the Life-Connection Process?
A **resistant mind** blocks the healing process with crystals, consciously or unconsciously. Some people may consciously want to heal and open themselves to this approach, but there may be unconscious resistance.

Depending on the amount of resistance we hold in our individual selves or in our family system (since our family soul and collective archaic consciousness may be too rigid), our movements to tune in, our surrender to allow the healing process to happen, and our willingness for the shifts to occur may happen in different proportions. There are many ways to release individual or collective resistance in energy healing, and the **CMLC** practices and techniques are designed for that if we commit to follow through with our part in the play.

Since as human beings we are naturally wired as creatures of habit, and habit is our comfort zone, when pain and suffering are habitual, they become "natural" to us. We "naturally" resist change because we are used to the distortions of our family history and our habitual limited thinking—even if it is good change, even if it is for a better life.

In our culture, we seem to be strangely addicted to emotional pain. It seems like we are biologically wired and inclined to suffer in one way or another, as if the neuropeptides of our cells and the cell of our bodies are in a state of "emotional addiction" (Tolle, 2008). This makes it more difficult for our conscious minds and commitments to deal with internal resistance and allow shifts to occur. Just knowing that shifts and changes are part of a natural flow of healing, however, may help us start to soften rigid resistance patterns.

In this perspective, **Cardinal Method of Life Connection** sessions and practices, like any other energy healing modality, or even allopathic treatments, will have stronger or weaker results in the proportion of each person's allowing or resistance of mind.

Three Ways of Allowing the Flow of Abundance in Our Lives

1. <u>Observe</u>: Are we living an authentic life, doing what we love and what we want, or are we fulfilling other people's expectations? Are our lives stagnant? Are we pleasers? Are other

people's priorities overshadowing our own? There is no such thing as imposed self-connection, but if we observe our lives and feel we are unhappy, we should not judge ourselves, and just observe life as it is and what are the best potentials possible, because life shifts all the time, and we can always connect to the abundant flow.
2. <u>Always choose life</u>: Connecting to life and allowing life to happen are simple, but difficult for those with a lot of unconscious distortions and a lot of resistance. If we commit to eliminate distortions progressively and surrender to the best of life, the abundant flow will take us. This happens faster when our hearts are pure and we release all past pain. With a pure heart, all good things flow to us.
3. <u>Trust</u>: When we start a life-connection process, even if part of us doesn't want to, we are already releasing distortions, stagnation, and resistance. If we start the process and then begin to resist, we must trust it is part of the challenge and keep going. We all have a dualistic aspect of the mind, and all spiritual efforts help to heal that. We must trust that the unintegrated aspects of the psyche will become more cohesive as we allow shifts to occur and never give up.

Purpose of The Cardinal Method of Life Connection
The purpose of **The Cardinal Method of Life Connection** is to encourage us to live in the free flow of life with as little emotional pain as possible, or at least using discernment to avoid unnecessary emotional pain. Pain is, of course, inevitable to some degree in life, but it can be part of our lives in smaller doses, while happiness and well-being become predominant. This predominance of happiness and fulfillment happens when we engage in any process of self-connection and spiritual growth (Ikeda, 2015).

Living the emotional aspects of life without being weighed down by inexplicable pain and discomfort is so much better. **The Cardinal**

Method of Life Connection uses the power of crystals to help harmonize relationships and allow us to become effortlessly more connected to our true selves, so we can live in more freedom and peace.

A good start to connect with this flow of happiness and well-being happens when we are aligned with our parents and observe what is our place and our size in our family. This means we must see our parents and ancestors occupying places in another hierarchy, higher than ours, regardless of their personalities. This will be elaborated in depth in chapter 3 of this book. When parents and ancestors are the "big people" in the family in our eyes, we are aligned with the functional level of consciousness at the collective soul level.

This is how we focus on the structure of the family, instead of deviating our attention to the personality of each member. Judging personalities is a distracting factor that confuses us and messes up our inner world. If our parents or grandparents behave like children, and the new generations feel emotionally forced to behave like adults and become emotional caretakers, this inverts the flow of energy in the family soul and creates energetic wounds and stagnation. This type of distortion is a heavy weight for the new generations to carry.

By aligning our individual perspective with our appropriate size and place in our families, we automatically relax and enjoy life a lot more. Simply by acknowledging that our parents and ancestors are in a higher hierarchical position within our family system, we make ourselves small and humble, which is a great relief for the soul. This is the structure of our functional consciousness, and it's better and smarter to align ourselves with this structure than to ignore it, or unconsciously rebel against it.

From a family constellation perspective, this is all it takes for life to flow in abundance and joy. From this fresh starting point, we can then expand our consciousness and develop more awareness of who we are. We also see others with more objective eyes, and naturally start living in a constant flow of inspiration. We are happy and fulfilled when we live from the sources of our truth and take the strength of life from our parents and ancestors.

By integrating our awareness and organizing generational hierarchy, **The Cardinal Method of Life Connection** encourages us to connect to the loving energy of our family members instead of living from their distortions, difficult personalities, and painful experiences. This choice will also align us and connect us to our life purpose. These are the greatest outcomes we will experience from living in our place and observing ourselves from the proportion of our size in our family system.

Practical Results from The Cardinal Method of Life Connection
Our minds create the reality of our lives. This is a fundamental principle in **The Cardinal Method of Life Connection**. We create the best life for ourselves when the real self and Higher or Spiritual Self attract our life experiences, and for that to happen, our minds must be healthy and clear. When the mind is unhealthy and unclear and carries many distorted contents, we cannot connect to our real selves, and the Higher Self cannot shine through as the creator of our lives experiences. When distorted contents in our minds create our path, we attract pain, suffering, unpleasant situations, and problems.

Whatever unpleasant situation we are caught in is happening because there are specific contents in our conscious or unconscious mind, such as belief systems and traumas, that are attracting these situations. The **CMLC** adopts a point of view in which the outside world is a mirror image of our inside worlds.

Knowing that whatever is going on outside of us is reflecting contents of your own conscious, subconscious, and unconscious mind, we have a choice to stop seeing ourselves as victims of the world. We go through challenges to learn from experiences and clear our minds of distortions, and when we clear the root causes of our problems, which are always within, shifts happen and life happens in a much better way.

Since the **CMLC** is a system designed to clear out these distortions in our minds and help us better understand ourselves and others, we will feel we are developing a clearer vision of what really matters once we engage in the process.

Cardinal Method of Life Connection sessions not only benefit us as individuals, but the energy also reverberates in our whole family as well. As a ripple effect, like when we throw a pebble in a lake, the healing that comes from this process echoes like expanding circular waves in the family soul. To some degree or another, consciously or unconsciously, every member of the family will feel the beneficial energy touching his or her life.

The **CMLC** healing energy will reach the areas of priority in the family, which are beyond our rational understanding and often surprise us. For example, a family member we rarely speak to may call us unexpectedly on the next day of a session for no reason and ask things that may be key to the healing we are focused on.

This clearly means a benign unconscious connection is always made with **CMLC** energy, and something shifts for all family members after a process. If nothing very explicit happens, it does not mean the energy shifts are not present. We never know what goes on beneath the surface, but we can be sure deep healing is going on at unconscious levels.

It is important to try not to analyze the process or the outcomes either. Rationalizing is a way the conscious mind finds to control, or even sabotage the healing, because the new shifts will break the old habits, and we tend to be afraid of change.

Talking to other people about **CMLC** sessions is not recommended either. Conscious silence is a great healing tool after a soul-healing process, and words are another way the conscious mind may try to use to control the situation and interfere in the energy; they become an unconscious self-sabotaging mechanism. Talking about a **Cardinal Method of Life Connection** session or a family constellation process weakens the energy, unless we are speaking to a practitioner in another healing session. Talking lightly breaks the healing power of the session, and most of the emotional effort will probably be wasted.

Respecting the silence required after **CMLC** process is a way to honor the work, since silence plays a huge role in healing after the process is concluded. Words in this sense weaken the healthy expression of emotions and are a way to not only avoid pain, but also to unconsciously resist change.

As far as results from sessions are concerned, if we respect conscious silence and trust that benign shifts will occur, we will feel a relief and a purification process in the most critical areas of emotional pain and relationship issues that block our happiness. These issues could be as simple as letting go of our distorted perceptions about members of our family, or as complex as radical change in our lifestyle, mindsets, inner world, and in the behavior of family members, professional colleagues, or our circle of friends.

Also, and most importantly, as our authentic self begins to surface and we become better at contemplating reality as it is, without reacting to it so much, we will start to experience major shifts as we progressively express our own truth. We will also see improvement in our health, well-being, and peace of mind, and gradually, we will experience more emotional freedom the more we commit to this life-connection process.

2

CRYSTALS

The **CMLC** uses crystals to shift the energies in our minds, and when we shift inside, the outside world, the environment, and other people around us shift as well. In a **CMLC** understanding, crystals eliminate distortions. Their high vibrational frequency elevates the vibrations of everything around it—including and especially our internal worlds and minds.

When we use crystals in a **Cardinal Method of Life Connection** practice, they are clearing out the distortions in our minds, souls, and emotions. When we clear ourselves, our relationships with other people and the outside world in general improve immensely.

Since we are creatures of habit, a lot of family souls have the habit of suffering. Crystal energy, however, is very joyful and very fun. Crystals will bring the family soul to a higher vibrational frequency of joy, as opposed to generations of painful emotional habits.

Crystals are structured bodies of matter with repeated internal geometrical patterns. In the healing field, they conduct electromagnetic energy waves, which are high vibrational frequencies that elevate the patterns of the energies around them. Each different crystal, depending on the shape and color, conducts a very specific type of vibration that can heal the soul and individual emotions in very specific ways.

The Cardinal Method of Life Connection focuses on the interaction between the crystal and the person who needs emotional and soul healing. This means we are focused on the emotional vibrations of the person receiving the session and how those vibrations can be aligned with a higher vibratory pattern naturally emanating from the presence of a crystal.

As said before in this book, for **CMLC** purposes you need to be constantly aware of these three basic aspects of a crystal energy in a healing field: the **geometrical structure** (the organizing aspect that strengthens our lives); the **colors** (the soul healing aspect that strengthens our lives); and the **sounds** that are made as inspired action to promote benign changes. These sounds are a combination of the crystal's abilities to irradiate sound vibrations (Hall, 2003) and the surrendering attitude we adopt as we speak words of affirmations, chant mantras, and say prayers that allow the flow of life and love to prevail in our lives.

Crystals have very precise healing toroidal energy fields that can benefit the emotional field, boost health because they lower the levels of stress, and increase well-being. A toroidal energy field derives from a torus-shaped movement of energy, which in geometry means a continuous revolving movement of energy that creates a ring around an object, or a donut shape.

This is what a torus looks like:

And this is an interaction between two toroidal energies:

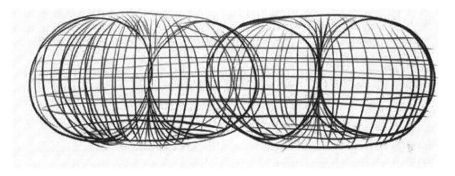

All units of matter (person, crystal, animal, plant, shoe, desk, or any given object or live being) has a torus field revolving around its central axle.

In a **Cardinal Method of Life Connection** session, the person's toroidal energy field activates the principle of similitude in specific crystals. This means that whichever aspect of the soul that needs healing will attract the specific crystal that can aid in that specific need, because their toroidal energies are compatible, and the crystal energy triggers the highest vibrations in that situation, which in turn, brings solution, neutralization, or harmonization. Therefore, the interaction between a person's story and a crystal in a **Cardinal Method of Life Connection** session can create relief, balance, healing, and release.

When someone choses a crystal to represent a person, an emotion, a place, a situation, a given problematic issue, or an energy in a **Cardinal Method of Life Connection** individual session, the crystal activates healing energies by following the principle "as above, so below." This means that "like attracts like," and that the highest vibrational frequencies (balance, love, life, joy) will prevail. This energetic magnetism expresses the principle of similitude and raises the vibrations of the situation at stake.

On the level of relationships, anything that is similar in two people's energy fields promotes attraction, even if it's not obvious to the conscious mind. This means we tend to attract friends and partners that are mirror images of some aspect of our psyches.

In a **Cardinal Method of Life Connection** session, the chosen crystals will bring the precise information and awareness, as well as the healing properties, for the specific situation or issue, and with the information, which relates to truth, healing and protection will follow when a crystal is present.

By choosing a crystal to represent something or someone in a session, we understand the energy or emotion that defines what is going on, because different crystals have different energies and heal specific patterns. Since like attracts like, what needs to be seen is revealed, and when we see the truth, healing occurs. This release protects us from vicious-circle patterns and painful emotional habits.

The interesting thing about crystals is that their presence aligns all energy fields as nature intended, and nature intended for life to be filled with joy, love, happiness, abundance, health, and well-being. On a relationship level, the energy starts to flow in spiraling patterns (fractals) of peace, love, harmony, understanding, joy, and life connection, which are what **The Cardinal Method of Life Connection** is all about.

The Seven Basic Crystal Systems
The science that studies **crystal systems** is called crystallography. There is no need to get very scientific about crystals when working with **The Cardinal Method of Life Connection** in individual practices, but if you want to research on your own, there are many books and websites on the subject (Thomas, 2008). In this case, not thinking in scientific terms can be a good strategy not to engage the conscious mind in the process and allow the emotions and the soul to take over the healing process.

You can find some individual practices in the book *Your Cardinal Connections* (Ramos, 2016). When you are healing yourself, the in-depth knowledge about mathematical and geometrical information is not required, and it might even make you lose focus from the emotional priority if what you are dealing with is painful. The conscious mind does that sometimes: it makes you pay attention to unimportant technical details as an excuse to avoid emotional challenges.

When working with others, however, you must be in as neutral an emotional space as possible and play the observer role. To become a **Certified Cardinal Method of Life Connection Practitioner**, you must know the basic geometric and scientific knowledge.

What you must first know about crystals is that there are thirty-two classes of crystals, and they are grouped in seven crystal systems. We will not explore the thirty-two classes of crystals in this book, but the seven crystal systems are important for the **CMLC**. Because of their different lattices, angles, and internal structures, crystal systems play distinct roles in healing in a **CMLC** perspective.

From a healing standpoint, these seven systems have different attributes and properties. This is because each crystal system creates a specific type of vortex, and vortexes are what provide the exact amount and type of healing and movement of energy in the family soul.

The technical details don't matter much in this phase of understanding, because at this point what really brings the shifts is our intuition. What guides us very precisely about what energy the crystal brings, or which crystal to pick for a specific issue, is always our intuition. In **The Cardinal Method of Life Connection**, this process is called **intuitive crystal connection**.

A lot of people do not study the scientific details of crystals, but they can establish very strong intuitive crystal connections regardless, because they know the crystal's basic spiritual attributes. I suggest you at least research the metaphysical aspects if you do not want to get scientific about it.

If you know the metaphysical information, and not the scientific, healing is very effective. When healing comes from someone with scientific knowledge, the technical information may help enhance the healing power of the session as long the focus is completely on the healing and integrates intuition, so it is not diverging into technical details of the rational mind.

In a **Cardinal Method of Life Connection** session, when we feel attracted to a crystal, we must always allow our intuition and feelings to speak first and guide our movements. Later we can do our scientific research to get the technical information (I suggest you do that, so that the right and left hemispheres of the brain are balanced and working in a dialect movement of synthesis).

You will be surprised every time you research the technical details, because the crystal energy will be exactly what was the priority for healing even before you had the knowledge. When you do the scientific research (which I recommended), you will be surprised with the "coincidences" between this knowledge and the practical situation you or the person you were dealing with are healing.

Observing the technical information about the crystal and the healing session brings expansion of consciousness, and as Judy Hall says (2003), crystals are the Earth's DNA, and the more you know about crystals, the more efficient they are. Because nothing in the physical world is static, and any mass of matter may seem static but is moving at the atomic level, crystals have specific energy frequencies because of their specific atomic vibrations (Hall, 2003). You can be sure—and I suggest you adopt this understanding—that rather than being static objects, every crystal, gemstone, or mineral you come in touch with is therefore moving vividly all the time.

The basic information about crystal systems is that there are seven of them, plus the "amorphous" group (which is not really a system, but an important category of classification). The seven basic structured systems are classified by their internal geometry, which is a symmetric, organized, constant and unchangeable atomic structure arranged in a three-dimensional format (Hall, 2003), with metaphysical healing properties. Crystals can be polished in several different forms and shapes, and their external format does not necessarily express their internal geometry. The external format adds geometrical information to a crystal, but that is secondary compared to the internal geometry.

The seven basic structured systems are divided into five quadrilateral systems, one hexagonal system, and one triangular system. All crystals encourage the energies of a good life, health, and strength to prevail over emotional distortions and destructive patterns, and their internal geometries help us align with these benign energies.

There are seven structured crystal systems in crystallography and one "amorphous" system, which includes crystals, stones, minerals, and natural resins without a geometric structure within. They have no geometric internal structure because these materials were either formed by the cooling of magma (like obsidian), solidified vegetable resin (such as amber), or solidified animal substances (such as seashells and pearls), or they came to Earth from the universe in the form of meteorites (such as moldavite). Even if they do not have a symmetric internal structure, amorphous crystals are nevertheless powerful tools to encourage the truth to come forward in a **CMLC** perspective.

The seven geometric crystal systems are isometric or **cubic; orthorhombic; tetragonal; monoclinic; triclinic; hexagonal;** and **trigonal** or rhombohedral. In the **CMLC**, the first three systems, which are more predictable and simple to understand, correspond to the first six chakras.

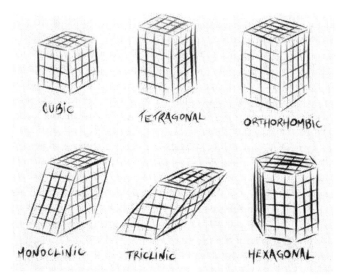

The trigonal system, which is pyramidal and has "unpredictable" angles, aligns the energy of the crown chakra.

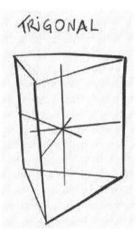

The **CMLC** correspondences do not limit the use of crystals on the chakras. It is a system of understanding and focus that enhances the healing power of crystals as they are aligned with specific chakra energy.

Crystals systems are important for the **CMLC** because they provide an interdisciplinary arrangement when connected to the Hindu chakra system. The **CMLC** uses not only the colors of crystals to align chakras, but also the internal geometry to organize our life paths in very specific ways.

For the **CMLC**, the cubic system in general organizes the energetic geometry of the root chakra; the orthorhombic system organizes the sacral chakra; the tetragonal system organizes the solar plexus; the monoclinic system organizes the heart chakra; the triclinic system organizesthe throat chakra; the hexagonal system organizes the third-eye chakra; and the trigonal system organizes the crown chakra.

Amorphous crystals do not have an internal structure, but they are important in a **CMLC** perspective, because the truth surfaces very quickly in their presence. An amorphous internal structure does not follow a geometric pattern, so it does not align energy, but it allows any distortion to be released from our internal world. The image below shows the difference between a crystalline structure and an amorphous structure.

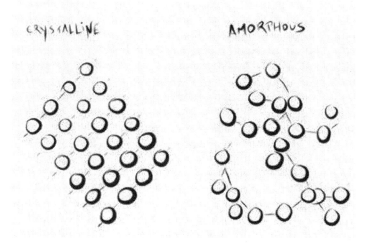

The **CMLC** perspective on the alignment of crystal geometries and chakras will be explained in more detail in chapter 7 of this book.

The presence of mineral deposits determines crystal colors. The nature of crystals determines their specific sounds (inaudible to people who have not developed a crystal connection), and the words we speak (sacred names, mantras, affirmations) are determined by our intentions to align ourselves with a higher purpose and higher vibratory frequencies.

Each crystal will intuitively and naturally be drawn to the field or chosen by the practitioner or the person herself to help with the process of healing the soul. In a **Cardinal Method of Life Connection** perspective, each crystal system has natural soul-healing attributes in their internal geometry. This means they are always working in a dialectic movement of synthesis between their own internal structure (thesis) and the specific energy in the environment (antithesis) to produce an optimal result (synthesis).

This creates healing that immediately creates a life connection in **CMLC** work. When we engage in this dialectic movement and raise our vibrational frequencies, we are healing not only ourselves, but also our relationships with ancestors, members of our families, circles of friends, and spiritual connections in a proportional and geometric way (Pacioli and da Vinci, 2014). Anything that is lacking or exaggerated will come into alignment because of the crystal geometry, color, and sound that begins to interact with a specific soul issue.

The interaction between crystals and an object, person, or environment is always a dialectic movement between two forces that create a higher vibrational outcome. Knowing this, you can trust the fact that crystals will always bring benign energies to our lives.

Internal Geometries, Colors, and Sounds
The Cardinal Method of Life Connection observes the healing power of crystals from their internal geometric structures, their colors, and their sounds, which cannot be heard by our physical senses. Sounds work as healing tools in the presence of crystals when we say affirmations, pray, or sing mantras in their presence. The sounds resonate with their internal geometries and realign our energy with benign currents and higher vibrational frequencies.

When we are observing specific crystal systems, it is important to train our minds not only to focus on the internal geometries, which align us in all directions of the three-dimensional physical world we live in, but we should also pay attention to how we feel when we are in touch with specific crystals. The more we learn about their internal geometry, the more we connect to them completely, and not only intuitively, encouraging our minds to develop mathematical and logical abilities. When our minds are stimulated by logical thinking, consciousness expands and we observe the world more objectively.

When we understand the dialectic movement of the internal geometry, the affirmations, and how this interaction reverberates in our inner world, we can trust benign results more firmly. When we train our minds and include technical information, and add the technical information to our feelings and intuition, we expand our consciousness and connect even further to the reality of all beings.

Spiritual Aspects of The Cardinal Method of Life Connection Crystals
As said before, the most important crystal attributes that constitute the fundamental principles of **The Cardinal Method of Life Connection** are the internal geometrical structure, the colors, and the sounds within and in the immediate physical environment the crystal is exposed to (for example, the words and prayers you say, or songs you sing, as you hold a crystal in your hand).

In Native American wisdoms, crystals *reveal the truth, heal,* and *protect* at the same time (Sams, 1990). Since many Native American cultures have polysemy, which means the same word is used to speak of many different things, truth, healing, and protection are part of the same concept. They walk hand in hand: where there is truth, there is protection and healing as well. In a **CMLC** perspective, knowing the truth automatically brings healing and protection to our lives, and to the energy of truth the **CMLC** adds love and joy as automatic properties of crystals. In practical terms this means no crystal, stone, or mineral has intrinsic negative energies. They absorb distortions to heal and protect living beings and environments (which is why they need to be cleansed).

When a person stands near or holds a crystal in a healing energy field, an accurate flow of information starts immediately. This is the energy of truth, healing, and protection the Native Americans talk about. When we receive this information, it is up to us to tune in or not. In the presence of crystals, the truth comes immediately and we choose to receive it or to engage in denial mode.

The information that comes through in a **CMLC** healing field reverberates instantly in the person's heart, mind, and whole body. You don't even have to think about it: you just know, absolutely, that the information you are tuning in to is true. In the **Cardinal Method of Life Connection**, this is called a "crystal-connection process."

Simultaneously, as the truth starts to surface, so do the energies of healing and protection that create and strengthen your consciousness expansion and allow you to know the best decisions to make and where to build healthy boundaries. In this crystal-connection process, you naturally begin to create healthier spaces for your life to flow, and as you move forward, for your consciousness to keep expanding.

The **Cardinal Method of Life Connection** also adds love, joy, and peace to this "truth, healing, and protection" triad, because when you connect to the energy of a crystal, you will feel it unblocks the flow of these other pure essences. These energies of truth, healing, protection, love, joy, and peace are precisely what creates life connection and brings healing to the soul. In the presence of crystals, the loving and healing energy of our Higher Selves (or spiritual selves) prevails, unless our minds have elevated levels of resistance.

For many Native American cultures, crystals, plants, animals, and humans are in the same hierarchy of natural living beings. However, while human beings hold a consciousness of separation—or a split mind between conscious and unconscious (Veltheim, 2011) for crystals, plants, and animals—dualism and separation between an individual being and the world do not exist.

In a **CMLC** perspective, forces of nature, crystals, plants, and animals do not hold complex intrinsic distortions of the mind as humans do. They are much more connected to life and to a pure state of being, or functional consciousness, than we are. Since they are more capable of maintaining their natural states of being and connection, whenever we humans get in touch with crystals, plants, and animals, we immediately align ourselves with a higher vibration of life and potentially keep ourselves tuned into higher vibratory frequencies.

Many traditional cultures live by this knowledge, so in their understanding, the closer we are to nature, the happier and the healthier we are, because we are connected. Animals, plants, and crystals help us live better lives in more constant connection to loving kindness, truth, healthy boundaries, clarity, and simplicity, and with a constant, natural ability to express our true authentic selves. When we are aligned with these energies, life, harmony, love, truth, beauty, and abundance prevail.

Purification: Crystals, Salt, and Water
In a **Cardinal Method of Life Connection** perspective, the best ways to clean, clear and cleanse your crystals is with either salt or flowing water (not salt-water solutions; use one or the other separately in their pure states). Cleaning a crystal is superficial, and we are cleaning the crystal surface. Clearing a crystal relates to the subtle energy that surrounds it. Cleansing a crystal is an internal process, which means we are cleansing the energy absorbed by the crystal in the spaces between the internal geometric structure.

There are crystal formations in salt and water (when water is in solid form). Salt crystals are very important for **The Cardinal Method of Life Connection** because salt is a neutralizer that brings bodies of matter to zero energy, meaning it neutralizes whatever energy content the crystal has come in touch with for healing. The crystallography name for salt crystals is halite (cubic system).

Water is also very important for the **CMLC** because *water is life*. Water cleans, responds to energy instantly energy instantly, flows (clearing your crystals under flowing water is better), and has a joyful, positive energy when in movement.

For the **CMLC**, water is very important for healing. First, in a **CMLC** perspective, all waters, and especially the oceans, can be considered a symbolic representation of the soul of the planet.

Second, as Dr. Masaru Emoto observed the "geometry" of water crystals (Emoto, 2008) and how water reacts to emotional energies. By forming either beautiful geometrical patterns when stimulated with good affirmations, or asymmetrical, distorted shapes when stimulated with negative affirmations, water responds immediately to creative energy, be it connected to life or destructive.

In Dr. Emoto's work, we contemplate images of beautiful water crystals that correspond to specific emotions or energies of higher vibrations. He has experienced the energy of joy, peace, prosperity, love, freedom, happiness, and many others. These energies and images can become references to improve health, vitality and well-being when intentionally used to charge water.

In the **CMLC**, since the molecules of our physical bodies are practically all made of water, when we associate affirmations with crystal geometry, the water molecules of our bodies respond immediately and vibrate in exponentially higher frequencies. In my years of experience with family constellations and **CMLC** sessions and crystals, I can say that something similar may be happening energetically in the family soul as well. The interaction of water molecules with crystals to create higher frequency and act upon emotional vibrations can be researched in further studies.

We can also use the images of water described by Dr. Emoto to see the family soul as if it were an ocean. As we use this analogous image of the family soul as an ocean, when something painful happens in the family that its members do not deal with—creating family secrets, trauma, and taboos—painful experiences of the past remain active and may be still reverberating. The soul becomes tainted and may have an unpleasant format and texture.

When higher vibrational frequencies of love, kindness, justice, expanded consciousness and awareness, protection of younger generations by ancestors, inclusion, and acceptance enter the soul through the heart of its individual members in a **CMLC** session, the healing creates a new reality in the soul and it shifts, becoming purified in a clearer, more crystalline state, more attuned with its original, natural geometric state.

Dr. Emoto's work should be observed for pointing out how healing natural, clear water can be. Not only because of the geometric beauty of water crystals, but also when we contemplate how water reacts to positive emotions.

This can be observed in a healing level of the physical body too, since about 90 percent of our human physical constitution is made of water. The water in our bodies will react and align with the healing energy in **CMLC** sessions. Crystals interact directly with the geometry of the water in our bodies. The alignment of the water in the body in a session will allow a better life flow not only to the person, but also to all those who are connected to him or her.

Concerning the crystalline nature of water on a scientific level, Dr. Pollack's researches about the "fourth phase of water" (2013, 2001) describes water behaving like a "liquid crystal":

To test whether the physical properties of the exclusion zone differ from those of bulk water, several methods have been applied so far. NMR, infrared, and birefringence imaging, as well as measurements of electrical potential, viscosity, and UV-VIS and infrared-absorption spectra, collectively reveal that the solute-free zone is a physically distinct, more ordered phase of water. It is much like a liquid crystal. It can co-exist essentially indefinitely with the contiguous solute-containing phase. Indeed, this unexpectedly extensive zone may be a candidate for the long-postulated "fourth phase" of water considered by earlier scientists. (http://faculty.washington.edu/ghp/research-themes/water-science/)

There are many ways to clean crystals, but in the **CMLC** I recommend you keep it simple and use salt or water, because their interaction with crystals is efficient and profound. The most recommended way to clear all crystals in a **CMLC** perspective is to lay them on a bowl of dry salt. We can put some salt over the crystals to cover their surfaces if we wish, as if we were burying the stones in the dry salt. We should allow them sit from five minutes to one hour, and they will be cleared. When we take them out of the salt bed, it is important to say a prayer or sing a mantra, and we will be good to go.

The reason dry salt is better than water is because it can be used with any stone, and some crystals dissolve in contact with water, such as tourmaline, selenite, and kyanite. They are porous, and water may penetrate and damage them. If the crystal is well polished and hard, though, we can put it for a few seconds under flowing water (which does not have to be a waterfall; it could be any faucet).

We will find recommendations to leave crystals in salt-water solutions or under the sun, but that is aggressive. In a **CMLC** perspective, this should be avoided. Salt water is corrosive, and sunlight will fade the color (unless it is a white or clear crystal). Sunlight is okay for any crystal if it is not exposed for more than five minutes.

Singing bowls, Reiki, sound healing, mantras, and prayers are very effective after you place your crystals on dry salt or under running water. Since salt is a neutralizer, after we clear crystals we need the first energies to come in touch with them to be of a higher vibration.

3

FAMILY CONSTELLATIONS

Collective Alignment of the Soul

Bert Hellinger is the creator of family constellations, a therapeutic modality technically known as Phenomenological Systemic Therapy of Bert Hellinger. Hellinger is a philosopher, a theology scholar, a psychoanalyst, and a psychodrama therapist. He used to be a Catholic priest of the Benedictine Order, and for sixteen years he was a missionary in South Africa, where he observed and learned traditional wisdoms about the human soul from the Zulu culture.

Hellinger's perspective of the soul combines Zulu wisdom, several approaches in psychotherapy, German philosophy, moral and ethical principles, and aspects of Christian theology. Much of Hellinger's method and therapeutic writings and practice about family constellations is based on the wisdom of the Zulus, so this makes family constellations both a multidisciplinary and a multicultural system.

General Family Constellation Principles

"Family constellation" is the common name of a very well-known healing modality for the soul. Technically, in German the actual word should be "placement" instead of "constellation," because it is about placing people in their correct spaces and correct sizes within a family system.

In a **Cardinal Method of Life Connection** interpretation, this gives family constellations a "geometrical" aspect because each one of us has a special, specific place as members of our families.. By "phenomenological" we understand that we do not "suppose" or assume anything before the actual experience of seeing the family field in a live constellation process. This means we do not assume anything and we do not draw conclusions before the process develops and reveals the root cause of the problem in that layer of consciousness.

The practice of family constellations is inspired by psychodrama. A group of people is joined together with the purpose of healing a story in someone's family system. Some of these people are chosen to "represent" members of the specific family, very much like in psychodrama therapy. We do not come to "the field" with any hypothetical assumptions, but with a concrete issue that needs a solution. In a family constellation perspective, the solution comes from being free from emotional identifications and "entanglements" with the past.

In a session, we allow the movements of healing to happen so that the story reveals itself. We look at the healing movements with "empty eyes" so as not to assume anything before the story unfolds. As we visualize the family's "emotional morphogenic field," or the soul of the family, the people in the group who are representing the family members tune in to the emotional frequencies of whom they are representing, even if they have never met the person before.

Real people who come to the group session will represent ancestors, family members, issues, energies, and significant others in the life of the person who is having his or her constellation. This representation of members must include all relevant individuals in a painful story, especially those who have been "excluded" from the "official family picture" (you will read more about this dynamic further in this book).

We need family constellation healing when often, as humans, our authentic selves are forgotten and we cannot access our inner truths because we are loyal to the pain of our ancestors, parents, aunts, or uncles. If one or several areas of our lives are not so great, there is a high chance we may be engaged in "family loyalty." These areas of life have little energy or may be distorted when we are constantly reacting to social pressure and painful and stressful experiences, which build up in our psyches, and we feel them as heavy emotional filters and distortions of perception.

What we do not realize until we include the collective soul perspective in the picture is that a lot of those filters and distortions are coming from the memory of our ancestors' emotions and painful life stories that are stored in our unconscious mind, and we have no idea that this is happening. When we realize that a lot of our pain does not come from our own individual experience, that emotional weight is released, and life takes a new route with renewed strength.

If "wounds in the soul of the family" have not been healed (this will be explained in detail later), we may experience our ancestors' pains as if it were our own experience. But from a family constellation perspective, it is indeed our experience, because we belong to the same system as our ancestors and share the same soul and collective unconscious mind.

However, even if it is part of our experience in a collective, panoramic level, it is not our individual story, and we must let go. Until that gets cleared out, we may suffer unnecessary emotional and sometimes physical pain (since a lot of diseases in the body, as seen in the records of family constellation professionals, may have to do with ancestral issues).

The family constellation perspective is that human beings have individual characteristics and individual behaviors, but most of our reality is unconscious and guided by a broader, stronger, collective force called the family soul. The family soul is like a fabric all members of a family are made of, and individual members are like embroidery in the generational tapestry.

In a **Cardinal Method of Life Connection** understanding, the family soul is a collective aspect of our psyches. Like icebergs, each individual human being is autonomous in her or his own individuality, but this autonomy is limited, like the tip of an iceberg above water compared to the larger body of ice underneath. Therefore, most of our reality is unconscious and submerged underwater, and we can't see it with our conscious minds, but it determines a great deal of our behavior and of our unconscious minds. In this perspective, we share the same unconscious mind and experiences of our family members.

Human beings belong to a collective soul with an archaic consciousness. The archaic consciousness is embedded in the functional consciousness level. The family soul follows what the archaic consciousness establishes as moral principles to follow. The most important soul principles are **hierarchy**, **belonging**, and **balance**.

Hierarchy versus Arrogance
The principle of hierarchy is also called "order" and expresses the flow of life in a generational, vertical alignment. This means that older generations have a hierarchical status compared to the next generation. Hierarchy or order are maintained in a family or business system when there is respect and gratitude to the elders.

In a biological perspective, Hellinger says human children are born poor and weak, and that parents and family members take physical care of us in the beginning of life by providing shelter and food until we are ready to survive on our own. Human children are born powerless and with no material resources. On a soul level, children are also born without wisdom. All we naturally and automatically have as children is innate love to give, which can be manifested as gratitude and respect toward those who brought us into the world.

When the natural love of the child is not used in the direction of gratitude and respect, but instead is manifested as judgment of parents and ancestors, the flow of life becomes a turmoil in the family soul, because the principle of hierarchy has been violated. When we judge our parents and ancestors and do not see them with respect and gratitude because of their actions and personality flaws, we create a wound in the soul and compromise the whole family system.

Hierarchy is therefore a principle in which those who are born in one generation have precedence over those who are born in a second generation, and so forth. When we violate this principle with our internal distortions, life is not as great as it could be.

Belonging versus Exclusion
The principle of belonging addresses the fact that no person and no aspect of a person can be excluded. Exclusion in family systems means family secrets, taboos, and forbidden subjects, among other issues. By making parts of the family history secret, or by judgment and condemnation of a person or situation, we create wounds in the family soul.

In a family constellation, all members must be included and acknowledged, so they can rightfully occupy their place in the family system. All members must be seen and included in the hearts of one another. It is a therapy that clears out exclusion, dishonor, and arrogance by welcoming, respecting, accepting, and consenting to the place, precedence, and size of each member within the system.

Hellinger considers that at least four generations share the same unconscious mind, meaning that the pain of these "immediate" ancestors is felt as our own pain even if it was not our direct individual experience. One of our ancestors or parents may have been a victim or someone who has caused damage to others in the past, and when there has been emotional pain in the family system, the soul knows. All members of the family know, even if we are not consciously aware of the situation. It is stored in our unconscious mind and may be playing a vital role in our lives without our conscious choice or control.

When something painful has happened in the family past and we are unconsciously judging that situation, we are dishonoring the hierarchy of positions. This is an unconscious attitude that always brings problems. It will be explained in detail later in this chapter, but in short, a dishonoring attitude means either judging an ancestor or trying to "save" and protect her from pain. When we try to save anyone, we are thinking of ourselves as bigger or better than the person who needs to be saved, even if she is no longer living and we don't even know her name, and even if she belongs to a prior generation and is bigger and older than we are.

The inner child sees only the emotional level of existence, and the only resource that child has is love. In the child's psyche, there is no difference between those who are alive today and those who have passed away. The inner child senses the painful experiences in the family's past and open wounds in the unconscious mind and is drawn to that space with an intention to remedy that situation. More about this will be explained further in this chapter.

Another way of dishonoring is by not validating parents or ancestors because of personality issues. If we want healing to happen, we must abandon that attitude and see that what really matters is the fact that our lives come from our parents and ancestors. That is larger than life itself because it is the strongest manifestation of love that is transmitted generation after generation and surpasses individual life spans.

When we see the structure of the family before we judge the individual personality of our parents and ancestors, we become small and can receive their strength. The size and the place of each member is respected before anything else, no matter how difficult the personality of that bigger person is (Hellinger, 2012).

Balance and Compensation
The principle of balance is when giving and receiving happen harmoniously according to the archaic consciousness of the soul, which is almost a biological phenomenon. Between generations—meaning parents and children, grandparents, parents, grandchildren, and so forth—all strength and resources must be given from the oldest generation to the newest generation.

Whenever there is lack in this flow between generations—for instance, when a mother is emotionally inconsistent and a child feels she needs to be stronger and take emotional care of her mother—there is an imbalance in giving and receiving. For the archaic consciousness of the soul, parents must be strong for their children, and not vice versa.

The principle of balance in giving and receiving is different in the same generation—siblings, husbands and wives, cousins—and in the social circles of our lives, between business partners and friends. The balance here must happen in a fifty-fifty ratio. Whenever we feel like we are giving too much in our professional, social, or romantic life, we are probably compensating for imbalances in our family system.

The distortion of compensation happens when younger generations try to take care of older members of the family, violating the principle of hierarchy, or when the fifty-fifty ratio in our relationships with partners, friends, and spouses is not respected. If these soul principles are disrupted, a wound is created in the collective or individual soul. The archaic consciousness, unconsciously shared by all family members, will create a compensation for that disruption.

There are many types of unconscious compensations for soul-principle transgressions. Compensations can be of several types, but something in the person's life, or in the lives of future generations, will collapse. For example, if a child's mother had an emotionally detached mother, this child will try to parent her own mother and may never create a healthy relationship with a partner for herself.

The Family Soul
Since the family soul is something we belong to in a family constellation perspective, a soul is collective in nature, and much larger than our individual lives and consciousness. The broadest conception of the soul is that we share the same soul with all our family members and with people from our culture too.

An image of embroidery on tapestry helps us visualize how things work on the collective soul level. We can think of the soul of the family as if it were the base of the tapestry, and each individual member of the family is a specific embroidery detail woven in this tapestry. If anything is "too tight" or not organized in any area of the tapestry, interfering in the "embroidery" (meaning a member of the family is in pain or experiencing negative emotions), the whole "fabric" is affected. If this member of the family is an ancestor, in one level or another it will affect future generations (this book has detailed information about this further along).

Since everyone is connected in a family for sharing the same soul, when one person goes through the process of a **Cardinal Method of Life Connection** session, all members of the family will benefit from the healing, since everybody in the system shares the same unconscious mind. The consciousness and awareness of one member brings healing to the whole soul in a ripple-effect mechanism.

Another image we can use to explain how this works is of icebergs in the ocean. You can picture icebergs floating in the ocean, and each individual member of the family corresponds to a different "iceberg." In this image, the soul of the family is the ocean. The icebergs are made of the same substance of the water in the ocean, only they are temporarily in solid form, and the soul in which the iceberg/individual is immersed is the fluid, in liquid form. An aging person can be compared to an aging iceberg melting in the water: as it melts, it becomes one with the family soul again.

The icebergs move with the currents of the ocean, and they also symbolize the proportion between conscious and unconscious mind, meaning most of the "reality" of our lives, like the iceberg, is submerged underwater. The visible tip of the iceberg corresponds to our conscious minds and is 3 to 10 percent of reality. This is very limited compared to the submersed mass of ice underneath the water, which corresponds to 90 to 93 percent, and even smaller if compared to the body of water of the ocean itself.

Identification with past pain occurs when one member of the family, in early childhood, becomes unconsciously connected to the life script of a family member who has suffered in the past. A family loyalty bond is formed, and this person may live the life script of an ancestor instead of connecting to his or her own individual life path. When there is identification with the life of an ancestor, there is great confusion in the individual mind of this person.

Love is indeed the source of life, and the real roots of family love (which is a very specific type of love) go much deeper than we tend to think. Also, family love reaches a lot more people than we can imagine, because the family soul is larger than we think. It includes both the living and the dead in the same status of importance, and it also includes those who have helped the family survive, those who have been part of romantic relationships with our ancestors, and all children, born and unborn.

The Cultural Soul
Now that we know that from a family constellation perspective, before we think of ourselves as individuals, we belong to a family system, it is important to point out we also belong to our cultures. In this perspective, before we think of ourselves as individuals, we are primarily expressions of two collective, previous forms of existence: the family soul and the cultural soul, and both family and cultural belonging deeply determine our subconscious and deep unconscious minds.

It easier to understand this new knowledge if we understand the concept of a morphogenic field, described in biology by Dr. Rupert Sheldrake (1995, 2013).

Morphogenic Fields
Like family constellations and many other energy-healing modalities, **The Cardinal Method of Life Connection** works within the scope of what Dr. Sheldrake calls a "morphogenic field." A morphogenetic field is

> a field of habitual patterns that links all people, which influences and is influenced by the habits of all people. This field contains (among other things) the pattern of that Japanese rhyme. The more people have a habit pattern—whether of knowledge, perception, or behavior—the stronger it is in the field, and the more easily it replicates in a new person. In fact, it seems such fields exist for other entities too—for birds, plants, even crystals. Sheldrake named these phenomena morphogenetic fields—fields which influence the pattern or form of things. (http://www.co-intelligence.org/P-morphogeneticfields.html)

In this perspective, a morphogenic field is always present whenever a person is present. Also, for **Cardinal Method of Life Connection** purposes, the presence of crystals acts deeply in the energy of a morphogenic field. First, their internal geometrical structure organizes the energy of the family soul. Second, their color resonates with specific healing vibrational frequencies within the soul in a **Cardinal Method of Life Connection** constellation session. Third, as we speak the words that allow healing to happen, those words not only resonate with the crystal geometry, but they also resonate in an organized pattern within the soul as an emotional energetic release.

A **Cardinal Method of Life Connection** session therefore provides shifts that bring alignment with love, health, and well-being within a person's morphogenetic field, or family soul. This is the reason **CMLC** sessions always include crystals to help heal painful issues, and sometimes to represent elements of our psyche in morphogenetic fields.

Something else is important when it comes to the presence of crystals in **Cardinal Method of Life Connection** sessions. In some Native American traditions (Sams, 1990), stones and crystals have the power to bring forth a threefold healing energy: **truth**, **healing**, and **protection**.

Also, since crystal systems have very specific internal geometric designs that align the morphogenic field to a natural, loving, healthy pattern, the family soul begins to align with this new, organized, healthy pattern as well. This means that crystalline structures encourage and enhance healing in morphogenic fields and align the subtle energies of an individual person (stagnant or distorted emotions, limiting beliefs, thought patterns etc.).

This is something that I have been observing in the last twenty years of my personal experience combining crystals with soul healing, even before I knew about family constellations. As a researcher of the natural and the distorted states of the soul, I know that if there is an intention and low levels of resistance to healing, crystals will help reveal the necessary information to highlight the distortions in the soul that need healing. Crystals will not only provide the information (bringing forth the truth) but they will also potentially activate the person's and the family's ability of self-healing. As Jamie Sams writes (1990), as the truth emerges, simultaneously it brings forth energies of healing and protection to all.

In a **Cardinal Method of Life Connection** session, you will experience this yourself. In the presence of crystals, very gently the precise information for what needs to be highlighted for healing to occur will naturally surface. This information will come to your conscious mind as insights, stories, memories, and inspirations for change and action. These insights will gradually bring more balance and healthy patterns of living to your life. The more you connect to the healing properties of crystals, the better your life will become.

The Archaic Consciousness of the Soul
In family constellations, the archaic consciousness is the shared unconscious mind of humanity, and family souls follow this shared unconscious mind. Both family and cultural souls share the archaic consciousness as a universal part of the human species, or human condition.

The archaic consciousness that guides family souls follows specific moral codes, and if individual members of a family disrespect theses moral touchstones, a wound is created in the family soul, and all members suffer to one degree or another, and the more sensitive, empathetic individuals may suffer more.

When we are unaware of the power of the archaic consciousness of the family soul, we might think we are autonomous and independent individuals. However, at the unconscious level we are more connected to the filters of past experiences of our ancestors and parents than we realize, and we often reproduce their ways of thinking, their belief systems, and their perception filters. We inherit everything from our parents' and our ancestors' experiences. They have been passed on to us through the DNA. Often, without realizing it, we live by repetition of ancestral and parental understandings and experiences, and not by our own authentic selves and inner truths.

All members of the family soul have the right to belong. However, not everyone is official and acknowledged as a member of the family. Those who are excluded exist in the family soul at a very intense vibrational frequency, and unconsciously, every member feels their presences, even if it is a family secret (for example, financial collapses, abortions, or violent episodes).

Even if consciously we are not aware of their existence, every human heart knows and sees the truth. There is no judgment of good or bad in the archaic consciousness, but there is judgment of right or wrong. In the unconscious logic of a family, only love and inclusion are recognized as righteousness, so if there are family secrets or taboos, the soul is being wounded.

Considering the cultural soul of each culture, which is superimposed upon the family soul, distinct cultural perspectives recognize certain situations in subjective ways. What is good in one culture is sinful for another (for example, polygamy). Cultural-soul moral values may vary in their standards of right or wrong, and so do unconscious collective judgments.

The Immature Love of the Child
Regardless of cultural moral values, in the perspective of constellations it is a universal condition for the human species that every time the truth is hidden, and/or a family member is excluded and

dishonored, the energy of that exclusion (be it an experience or a person) will be represented in the family soul in future generations.

Children are sensitive and feel the truth very strongly. They have no power and no wisdom—all they have is love, and their love is "blind" and "immature," because a child thinks he or she can compensate exclusion by living the same experience, thinking he or she can have a different, successful outcome.

For example, if a grandmother has suffered domestic violence from her husband and has never spoken about it, even if it is not an official story, a granddaughter will feel that that pain as if it were her own. This granddaughter becomes identified with the painful experience of her grandmother and may repeat the same story in her own life as a (useless) effort to share the pain in family loyalty.

The immature love of the child makes us feel as if we can either "save" a parent or ancestor, or avenge them, by unconsciously attracting similar situations to our individual experience.

Once children sense the truth of exclusion and dishonor in their unconscious mind, they are likely to try to compensate for the pain by "taking care" of the unfair situation for their ancestors, or even of siblings. For example, if a child is born after her mother had an abortion or miscarriage, this child may feel "the guilt of the survivor," thinking it is not fair that she was born and her own brother or sister wasn't. This child may never fully embrace happiness to compensate for the pain of an unborn sibling, feeling unworthy of life and guilty for being born when her sibling was not.

This innocent behavior of a blind, immature love is a fantasy in the mind of a child, but is more common than we think in the inner world of adults who are unconsciously entangled in the systemic wounds in the family soul. The immature love of the child may be secretly ruling our lives without our knowing it. It is potentially more active than we realize.

Since in the unconscious mind of the family there is an active energy of pain, a "family wound" that is not limited to time or space, the child within may unconsciously become representative of excluded or dishonored members of the family system. They connect to an emotional programming and try to "save" wounded family members by repeating similar situations in their lives and unconsciously finding a way to stay close to them.

In this perspective, one of the major problems of the human experience may be that by identifying with painful experiences of ancestors, parents, or siblings, many people do not know where they belong. They get confused about what is their place and their size in the family system, where they should stand, and what is their path.

They tend to have less life force and generally may lack energy in their lives because they are not standing in the optimum place to take all the strength they can get from their parents and ancestors. Instead, they are dwelling in the family soul, unrooted, engaged in the immature love of the child, and identified with other people who had painful experiences in the system.

When we are entangled in reediting these painful family experiences through emotional identification for the sake of family loyalty, representing the excluded members or situations, we do not honor the life we have.

Consenting to Life and Connecting Our Love to Personal Power and Wisdom
Honoring our own lives is only possible when we abandon the filters of the immature love of the child, which blinds us from the reality of the present moment and disconnects us from the benign,

natural flow of life. We abandon the immature love of the child when we consent to what is, accepting life as it is instead of reacting to whatever happened in the past that is not ideal. When we do that consciously and willingly, we stop trying to interfere in the past and to take care of what is not our business, because it belongs to other, higher hierarchical levels of the family soul. It is not our problem to solve.

On a systemic level, the archaic collective consciousness of the soul tends to follow principles of justice and compensation, so we do not always have unanimous aspects of consciousness within our psyches. To this archaic consciousness, whatever was excluded from the family soul will become the gravitational center of the unconscious mind of future generations until it is seen, included, and honored.

From a conscious-mind perspective, this may not seem fair to the new generations, because they will be entangled in the family's painful past—not because of their own doings, but because of ancestral or parental stories.

If issues remain hidden and unresolved, from an archaic consciousness perspective, it becomes a "black hole" in the family soul that will attract one or two or more children in the family system, who will be entangled because we are born in the immature, blind love that knows no personal power and no wisdom.

If any member of the family disrespects hierarchy, the right to belong or balance in giving and receiving in the past, and that remains as an open wound in the family soul, someone in the new generations will compensate for it (Hellinger, 2012).

Family-soul healing comes from seeing and including the truth, consenting to the reality of what is, and remaining in our places and our sizes in the family system. When we are not emotionally "arrogant" in the effort to save family members who are in a higher hierarchy than us, or trying to solve situations that were caused by our parents and ancestors, we are not entangled.

This can be hard in certain family systems, especially when the big person in the story—a parent or ancestor—has an inconsistent personality and does not take responsibility for his or her actions. Children get very confused with parents or grandparents with an inconsistent, childish, or irresponsible personality. This will likely lead to a situation in which a child will become entangled in emotional efforts to try to solve problems that are none of his business and feeling responsible for things that belong to older people in the family soul.

The innocent love of the child and the attempt to compensate for wounds in the family soul are triggered when a member was wounded, excluded, wronged, injured, or killed, or had a premature death that has not been fully accepted or honored. When these painful experiences happen, the family soul is wounded, and sensitive children tend to compensate for the damage.

Children who come into wounded family souls tend to sacrifice themselves with painful experiences as an effort to "save" family members from their suffering, drawing similar paths of pain toward themselves. Isolation, mental disorders, money losses, violence, abortions, relationship problems, and inability to hold a job are some examples.

Hellinger's perspective is that the archaic unconscious mind of families does not follow concepts of goodness and compassion, but instead, it is connected to concepts of truth and justice. The best thing an individual member of a family can do in this scenario is to take responsibility for his or her own actions to protect future generations from becoming unconsciously identified with family pain. This means honoring and including all members of the family and not treating painful situations as taboo and keeping family secrets.

Those who are caught in family entanglements begin to heal when they replace "the immature love of the child" for the "mature love of the adult" (Hellinger, 2012). This means, in a **CMLC** perspective, that there is a quantum leap in the person's individual psyche when he or she consents to all the painful memories of the family without judgment and allows what belongs to ancestral hierarchies to rest in peace.

By releasing the past and connecting to the present moment, we stand where we belong in the family system—in the correct place and proportional size, connected to our own individual life paths, instead of repeating the past painful experiences of our ancestors, parents, aunts, or uncles.

The family soul does not judge experiences with ideas of good or bad—it does not know these concepts because it only recognizes structure, and not personality traits. The deep love of the family soul recognizes hierarchy, the right to belong, and balance in giving and receiving. The idea of someone being good or evil does not mean much to the family soul.

What matters is if this person belongs, where the person belongs, and if the person is being honored. No matter what kind of personality she had, what matters is that she has a place in the soul, and when all family soul members honor the excluded ones, there is healing, and there is peace.

It would be pretentious to think we can completely access all the stories of our family history, but when we understand these three soul principles, we can focus a lot more on our own lives and bring new and beautiful things to the world. When we honor and release the past, we move toward the truth of our own hearts and engage in the present moment in a very powerful life connection.

Loyalty to Painful Experiences
Painful experiences or "wounds in the family soul" most frequently come from exclusion, hierarchy defiance, or imbalances in the giving and receiving. On an unconscious level, all members of a family know and feel the truth but are not officially aware of the truth when there are family secrets or taboos (forbidden subjects).

Excluded members of the family are lovers, parallel families, children who were not born (abortions or miscarriages), and family secrets in general. However, on the emotional level, there are no secrets, and it is painful for the soul to feel something that is part of it is excluded, and many of its individual members do not consciously and openly know what the truth is.

Individual Responsibility and the Dialectic Movements toward Freedom: Two Ways to Love
As I have said before, the immediate collective soul we are embedded in is the **family soul**, and we also belong to a **cultural soul**. These collective souls behave in accordance with an archaic consciousness that follows principles of **hierarchy**, **belonging** and **balance**.

These principles are considered "orders of love." They are expressions of "collective soul love," not ego love or inner-child love. When the inner-child love sees the truth and understands the big picture (its antithesis), it engages in the mature love of the adult, the synthesis of this individual dialectic movement.

The love of the child and the love of the ego are self-centered and focused not on the other person, but on trying to heal one's own wounds, on judging others for problems in the family, and on looking at the past. Inner-child love is immature, and ego love is proud and vain, and both are arrogant in their fantasies (child) and judgment (ego). The love of the soul described here acknowledges all members of the family as equally important.

Healing and Alignment
That way, healing in a family constellation or **CMLC** session is about

1. making ourselves small, which means we bow to our parents and ancestors, abandoning all judgment of their life stories and personalities;
2. honoring and thanking Mother and Father for our lives;
3. allowing them to take care of us in the forward direction, instead of seeing ourselves as superior to them and trying to take care of past issues in the inverted direction.

If parents and ancestors have personality problems and have hurt us consciously or unconsciously, they do not correspond to an ideal parent or ancestor, but it is the reality of life and not a perfect-world scenario. Most **CMLC** family constellations and **CMLC** individual sessions tend to be about personality issues and destructive attitudes of parents and caretakers that interrupt the flow of love—and life—in the system when we are children, or when our parents were children, or when our grandparents were children, or all the above.

When we see where the love flow was interrupted in a session, we can solve to some degree the "family entanglement" and reactivate an energy of protection and integrity that is the source of our inner strength. In that perspective, the search for harmony with Father and Mother and the personal choice to move on and surpass the conflicts with their personality traits is not very different from the work of Sigmund Freud. And it can also be a stepping stone to what Carl Jung called "The Process of Individuation" in his work (1968).

Concerning similarities to Freud and Jung, Hellinger's vision includes the two basic concepts of making peace with Mother and Father and moving forward in the process of becoming an autonomous individual. However, when it comes to the strength of the unconscious mind, Hellinger's approach focuses on something significantly different.

While Freud states that an individual's unconscious mind is mostly influenced by issues related to Mother and Mather, and Jung has developed the idea of a collective unconscious mind of humanity inhabited by universal archetypes, Hellinger observes something in between: the perception that we belong most strongly to a family unconscious mind that includes aunts, uncles, grandparents, and great-grandparents, and to a cultural and ethnic unconscious mind.

For Hellinger, the ultimate truth of the human condition is that we are members of a collective family soul that speaks more loudly than any other type of group belonging. This family soul, as it was already mentioned, is shared by all individuals in that family system, and its wounds are expressed through its members and felt by all of them to one degree or another.

When a member of the family is or was in pain, all members are in pain. It affects the whole group, and especially when it comes to linear ancestors (great-grandparents, grandparents, parents), we feel it as if it were our own individual experience. And when we unconsciously do not understand or we judge the painful experiences of other family members, we become entangled.

A family constellation is therefore a therapy that intends to soften or release these entanglements, and so is the **CMLC**. When each member of the family is in his or her right place and right size within the system, all members experience peace. A family system is disorganized when one or more members are identified with the painful life experience of ancestors or excluded members, and leave their birthplace to occupy or to be next to the members of the family who have gone through painful experiences.

The solution to this in a family constellation or **CMLC** session is to see and consent to what has happened in a family and move on, focusing on the fact that the present has priority in relation to the past. It's a great relief that allows life to flow forward. When each member of the family and the past are respected, and each member occupies his or her rightful place, life begins to make sense again.

If we honor and respect our ancestors, the strength of life we have received from them is greater than all limitations, once you go through this self-connection process you will become less attached or guided by this archaic consciousness. You will become less judgmental and will stop carrying a lot of the unconscious emotional weight of your family system. You will begin to live your life at its full potential naturally, because you will get rid of a lot of the filters of your family system.

We stop trying to find fault in our parents and ancestors. Instead of judging them, we become grateful for the life that has been given to us and start to see things in a clearer perspective. We realize we should honor and thank them for what really matters in life, which is greater than any pain that has been passed on throughout generations.

When we start to think that way, we release our hearts from conscious and unconscious burdens and connect to our truths. We start acting more according to our loving nature and inner wisdom. When we honor our ancestors and parents, we become whole and live more authentically. This connection allows life to unfold in unlimited movements of energy and love. We also become more receptive, instead of being so reactive, to shifts and changes. We begin to realize that shifts and changes are aligned with life's natural constant flow. We start to live happier lives in healthier bodies, constantly growing and healing while accomplishing our individual life purposes.

Soul Alignment
As far as healing of the soul is concerned, one of Hellinger's most important insights is the idea that modern Western perspectives of individuality are not enough to explain the human condition or the human psyche. Individuality is an important aspect of the self, but we are also made of deep collective identities that form our unconscious levels of being. In family constellations, these are called "systemic bonds" that connect us to remote ancestors many generations back. These systemic bonds also give us a deep sense of belonging that surpasses individual identity, even if we are not consciously aware of it.

The fourth and seventh prior generations are major sources of healing for us as individuals, and in the **CMLC** experience, healing does come especially from these two prior generations. We do not live in such independence and autonomy as we tend to think, but we are not completely helpless in the family system either. The wounds may come from prior generations, but so do the keys to healing.

In Zulu wisdom, before you think of yourself as an independent individual, it is important to realize you are primarily part of this collective soul—family and cultural identity. Before you say your name, you have a family name and a cultural background that define you much more than your individual sense of self. Therefore, we are "collective beings" prior to being individual persons (which we also are, but this sense of individual self is developed later as part of the evolution of each human journey).

In the Zulu culture, individuals are respected and "seen" as members of a family, and that whole family is treated with profound respect when the individual person is addressed in any given situation.

That way, when a Zulu person says, "I see you" to another person, he or she sees the bigger picture and treats the individual as if the whole family were present—the "you" is collective, meaning it includes the specific person and all ancestors behind this person, especially mother and father, grandparents, and the family lineage. So "I see you" means "I see you, your parents, and your grandparents behind them, and your great-grandparents behind them," and so forth.

Influenced by the Zulus and incorporating Western philosophy and theology to this healing modality, Hellinger agrees that human beings are not solely individuals. In his perspective, we are indeed all part of something bigger than our own individual selves. In this approach, each human being is a manifestation of the broader, collective reality called "the soul" and when that is embraced, life begins to change.

Since the soul is a shared entity that moves in time and accumulates experiences, all family members as individuals belong to it. Sharing the same unconscious mind, the same feelings, the same emotional frequencies, the same experiences on some level of the deep unconscious mind can reveal the roots of many emotional and even physical problems.

As I said before, in this context, "individuality" is a place where each person stands within the soul of the family system. And we all have a very specific place where we belong and from where life flows to us (I will later explore further explanations about how this can get complicated). This is especially important if a person has siblings who were not born and thinks he may be the first child of his parents, but though he is the firstborn, he is literally the fourth biological child, which has a different place in the matrix or geometry of the family system.

The impact of this "mathematical" order is huge in the family soul and in the heart of the individual. People get very confused about the emotional and unconscious levels when this sort of misplacement happens. A lot of healing comes from just knowing our exact spot and where we truly belong in the order of our siblings. Some siblings may have been born and some may not, but as far as the family soul is concerned, all siblings, being born or otherwise, exist and belong equally.

Aside from Zulu wisdom, Hellinger says something that is extremely important when it comes to healing, self-connection, and spiritual growth. It is like many references in Christian theology and very compatible to St. Augustine's idea of soul distortion and free will (St. Augustine, 2017).

Arrogance
Hellinger's idea of arrogance may come from a theological inspiration in the idea of free will. This makes his work very interesting because it combines traditional wisdoms from South Africa with Western theology and references from German philosophy such as the work of Immanuel Kant (when he talks about immature and mature love) and Friedrich Hegel (when he talks about dialectics). This makes Hellinger's work apt to be qualified as applied philosophy as well as a therapeutic modality.

As far as Kant is concerned, in Hellinger's idea of arrogance, we make choices to live either in the immature love of the child, in Hellinger's words, or we can live according to the mature love of the adult. In Kantian terms, the latter may correspond to the idea of "self-determination in the age of Reason" (Kant, 2002).

Hellinger says that as individual members of the human species, each single human being on the planet tends to be arrogant, on a conscious or unconscious level. And all the problems in our lives have that exact same root: we are consciously or unconsciously arrogant in our family system.

Our arrogance can come from judgment of parents and ancestors, disqualifying their personality traits, or from the immature love of the child who has the fantasy of taking care of issues that belong to the past by reediting them in their lives. When we live from unconscious arrogance, it means we see ourselves in a distorted way in the panorama of the family soul: as if we are morally superior compared to our ancestors, as if we could change the past through our present lives, and as if we could take care of things that are, in truth, too intense and too heavy for us to handle.

Arrogance blinds us in the illusion that we can change the past by unconsciously repeating our ancestors' experiences to make things right in our own experience, and by doing that we disconnect from the flow of life that moves forward and become entangled in the family system.

The Love of the Child and Family Loyalty
An example of the immature love of the child would be a woman who has emotional issues and cannot sustain long-term relationships. She may be unconsciously "identified" with a painful marriage of an ancestor—say, her grandmother. This grandmother was not validated by her husband (the woman's grandfather) and may have been often spanked by him. This was very likely a family secret, which may emerge from **CMLC** or family constellations, or other modalities of energy healing.

The problem is, there are no "secrets," because all members of a family share the same unconscious mind—the family soul. This contemporary woman who cannot sustain long-term relationships may unconsciously engage in painful love affairs, in which she is repeatedly hurt emotionally or even physically abused.

What is really happening is that she may be unconsciously engaged in what Hellinger calls "family loyalty." This is not something we consciously choose. It is a tendency we all have, in some degree or another, when there has been a lot of pain and suffering in a family system. Family loyalty is therefore a way to feel closer to her unhappy grandmother, and unconsciously comfort her, even if it causes the contemporary woman, her descendant, unnecessary suffering.

This is not a conscious or rational choice, but it makes sense emotionally in the perspective of the immature love of the child. It is still love, and love is the most natural energy of our human condition.

When we are living in the immature love of the child, it means we do not accept the fate of our ancestors and family members. We do not accept the pain of the experiences and desperately try to "fix the past" in the immature, arrogant illusion that, as descendants, there is something we can do about it.

We may then in vain try to repeat similar painful situations or to be sympathetic with them by sacrificing part of our lives to suffer together with them. This is also an unconscious way to alleviate the guilt of having a great life when in the past our ancestors have suffered so much.

The healing of the soul can happen when you engage in the other option of love, described by Hellinger as the mature love of the adult. This type of love consents to what is and does not unconsciously try to "save" family members from their misfortunes by making personal sacrifices to feel like them in their suffering. So the key to engage in the mature love of the adult is to consent to reality as it is and as it was, and move on with our lives.

Once you understand your unconscious movements (which become very clear to you once you have a **CMLC** or family constellation session with a certified professional practitioner), you can abandon automatic, destructive, unconscious behaviors and engage in more authentic, spontaneous, and free lifestyles and life choices.

The key to understanding Bert Hellinger's perspective is to embrace a new point of view about individuality in the human condition, meaning we are not autonomous, independent human beings, but rather, we are part of collective souls, and we largely express the soul of our families of origin. We share the same unconscious mind as our ancestors, and their experiences are, in a way, our own experiences as well, though we have not lived them directly. They are imprinted inside of us and constitute our bodies, our cells, and our minds.

That is precisely the perspective of the **CMLC**. Our human condition has a collective nature that coexists with an individual, unique singular aspect we call the self. The collective aspect of our being may interfere in our individual selves and change the direction of our unique life paths. If that happens, we may not become who we were born to be because we may be "entangled" in painful past experiences of our ancestors.

If that happens, it is because the immature love of the child keeps looking back at the downfalls of ancestors and instead of moving ahead, desperately tries to save them. This has been said before by many other schools of thought on an individual level—the inner child recreates painful experiences of his or her own life by mimicking painful experiences lived with the parents to finally "win the game."

However, if we see ourselves as collective beings, we know that we immediately belong to a family soul that rules our unconscious mind. We may then recreate not only our own painful childhood experiences with Father and Mother, but also past experiences that have happened long before even our parents were born. Hellinger says we may be reediting issues from four to five generations past, but in the **CMLC**, we can easily trace back seven generations with the proper techniques.

This condition of "belonging" to our family of origin is the starting point for the family constellation perspective: understanding that we have a collective soul and that our individual spirit begins to act in the world from the perspective of this shared soul that belongs to all family members. In a **CMLC** perspective, until we turn twenty-one years of age, we tend to be more "systemic" than individually independent, meaning we are unconsciously living from the archaic consciousness of the family soul more than from our own minds—if there are a lot of unsolved issues in the family past.

Our family of origin is the result of the previous two family systems: the father's birth family and the mother's birth family—which usually mirror each other in painful experiences if we look closely. This means there are usually similar problems and issues in both our mother's family and our father's family. Throughout life, we also create our own nuclear families and tend to marry people who come from family systems that are on some level like ours.

We also belong to several other social, professional, and cultural groups. As in families, any group that is formed also has an unconscious and shared soul that influences us to a minor degree. Further information about social groups and non-blood-related shared consciousness can be observed in what Hellinger calls "organizational constellations," which are not the purpose of this book, but will be further explored in future **CMLC** publications.

In the perspective of family constellations, **CMLC** sessions work by unfolding layers in the family's morphogenic field. The person is exposed to the family morphogenic field and consciously expands awareness in going from the immature, blind love of the child, identified with systemic entanglements, to more authentic and expanded manifestations of the true individual self.

We see people moving toward their place of right within the family system. However, different from Bert Hellinger's original therapy in which relatives, emotions, and energies are represented by actual live people (as in Moreno's psychodrama techniques), **CMLC** sessions consist of using crystals to represent family members, energies, issues, symbols, abstract figures, and emotions.

By committing to the idea that as human beings we are our own individuality but much of what we are also consists of family belonging, the **CMLC** incorporates principles of family constellations that do not deny individuality, but extend its scope to the idea that each person is an expression of self, ancestry, family, and even of culture and country.

Since in Hellinger's view, all humans are primarily collective and live from their places in the system, individuals can express themselves, but the fact is that family systems precede individual consciousness. Before we think of ourselves as individuals, we must think of ourselves as expressions of the family soul, and authentic self-expression can only be fully manifested if the person is aligned with his or her place in the system.

To be aligned with your place in the family system is, in turn, to follow the orders of love and organically grow from one circle of life into another exponentially (this will be explained in detail in the following topics of this chapter). We follow the orders of love and grow into the circles of life by honoring our parents and ancestors and by not being involved in the entanglements of family origins.

All these aspects constitute the basic foundations of The **CMLC** in the scope of family constellations and its guiding principles.

Individual self-expression can therefore be considered a form of freedom, and it exists only when the individual relates to the world by being connected to the essence of the family soul and not living according to unconscious reactions to family pain. This allows us to live from the heart, and when that happens we do not represent family members and do not repeat painful experiences. We stop reviving the emotions and life scripts of previous generations and engage in self-connection to live a fulfilling life.

The Soul as an Environment or Geographic Area
In a **CMLC** perspective, it is easy to visualize the soul as a geographic area. The closer an individual member of the family is to a "transgression" or "soul wound," the higher the probability of this person collapsing in his or her individual life. However, the movements of the soul are not obvious, and collapses can skip generations, or they can happen in a "diagonal line." For example, it is possible to see children identified with painful experiences of aunts and uncles, who are not directly related to them in a vertical line.

Try to think of the soul in a geographic or topographic image. If a person stands where there is a soul wound in that geography or topography, that person may likely repeat the painful situation in his or her own life.

Levels of Consciousness and the Dialectic Movement of Life
To understand Hellinger's approach, it is important to comprehend the dialectic movement of life in our own personal experience. This is not as complicated as it sounds—it is very simple and can be addressed here as "applied philosophy." Dialectics is basically a

three-step movement in which we have a thesis, an antithesis, and a synthesis. Each one of these three elements, when balanced, constitutes a movement that overcomes obstacles and continuously takes life to higher levels of consciousness, love, and abundance.

The **CMLC** considers that the three levels of consciousness to be explained follow a dialectic movement, meaning each new level or step does not exclude the former, but rather incorporates it and transcends it to a higher and more expanded degree (which is what dialectic movements are about). This is crucial when we are trying to understand emotional suffering and how to get out of it, if that is our wish.

In Hellinger's philosophy, each human being, as an individual, is "permeated" by three distinct types of consciousness: **group consciousness**, **personal consciousness**, and **universal consciousness**. For the **CMLC**, this would correspond to **functional consciousness** (which embraces cultural moral values and the collective consciousness of the family soul), **individual consciousness**, and Higher Consciousness.

Hellinger sees these levels in a dialectic movement (thesis, antithesis, and synthesis). As we rise to higher levels of consciousness, the ongoing dialectic movement never eliminates the former level; it integrates it and transforms it into strength to move forward to the next level to come.

The first and most primitive type of consciousness, in this perspective, is group consciousness. It is a given of the human condition, and no one can escape it. Group consciousness in Hellinger's terms can be roughly described as an almost instinctive "collective orientation for survival," which we belong to and are part of. In this level of consciousness, we are unaware of our individuality and feel our existence as if all that we are is the group.

In that sense, the strongest manifestation of group consciousness is the family system, but cultural bonds are also very strong. As I said before, both family and cultural belonging are stronger and precede individuality.

On this level, if there has been dishonor in the family—exclusion, pain, and suffering that have not been completely processed by the soul—individuals in the new generations suffer, and their conscious minds are not aware of the source of the problem. The new generation simply feels the pain, and its members collapse, struggle too much in life, and may even have survival issues because they are entangled in family loyalty—which means they are expressing the pain until it is seen and honored.

The second type of consciousness is personal consciousness. It emerges from interpersonal relations among social groups. Interpersonal relationships allow something new to emerge, which does not eliminate group consciousness but coexists with it. This expansion of consciousness is called personal consciousness, and it creates an organic movement of life toward a perception of an individual self.

Not all people understand or develop this level of individuality, especially if people belong to afamily-based or very traditional - culture. Developing a sense of self requires dedication and connection to what is authentic within, an effort of self-connection and self-discovery. This is not a step everybody wants to or can take. Many times, we are simply expressing the family soul without developing a sense of self, and there is nothing wrong with this, but collective consciousness and personal consciousness are two very different aspects of the human condition.

The third type of consciousness is universal consciousness. For Hellinger, it began to develop itself with the migration of cultural groups and the contact with cultural differences, which paved the way to the development of a universal consciousness of humanity. Many expanding cultures have developed this type of consciousness in the past but not all present social groups or present individuals have come to or are interested in this level of consciousness. It requires compassion, acceptance, harbor, and honoring of others, without the "selective affections" of family members. If it's hard to even give all members of our own families a place in our hearts, imagine including all of humanity. But for Hellinger, this can be a reference to the evolution of the human condition.

Movement of the Soul and Image of the Tree
In the **CMLC**, we see the three levels of consciousness as if they were part of the same tree: collective group consciousness represents the roots, personal consciousness represents the trunk, and universal consciousness represents the branches, leaves, blossoms, fruits, and seeds.

This image means we are out in the world and could be developing as many harmonious and healthy relationships as possible, like expanding branches of a tree. To reach personal and universal consciousness, individuals need to fully take the strength from the parents and family systems ("roots")—otherwise they will remain entangled in the collective group consciousness, and life, health, and well-being will never be manifested in their full potential as they could be.

It is important to understand that in this image, the roots represent our ancestors and all the strength that comes from our collective, primitive, archaic consciousness. The trunk represents our parents and our individual selves (who build our personal consciousness); and the leaves, flowers, fruits, and animals that live in the tree are an expanded life that reaches out to universal consciousness when we do our job to fulfill our life purpose. The more we take the strength from the roots, the stronger the trunk, and the more beautiful the branches, leaves, flowers, and fruits.

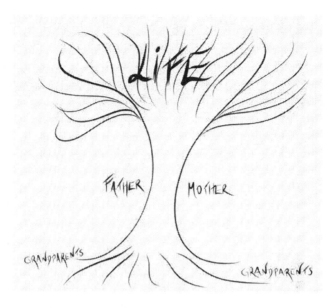

Orders of Love

In a family constellations perspective, love can only flow within an orderly framework; otherwise it creates chaos and entanglements (Schneider, 2007). The orders of love are what we can also call "moral laws of human nature" in the **CMLC**, but they do not stand as commands or obligations—they depend on our free will, and that should be respected. It is important to know that our inner wisdom and our spiritual growth are expressions of love and are always very kind. They do not rush or threaten us in any way. When we choose to follow the orders of love, we reach the entry points to healing and to a good life.

What Bert Hellinger calls "orders of love" are a set of healthy emotional choices that connect us to our ancestors and at the same time allow us to connect to our life purpose. However, when we do not make room for these orders of love in our lives—when our love is not in the flow of these orders, there is disorder. We may experience discomfort on some level, be it emotional, physical, financial, or any other area of our lives. Our energy field becomes chaotic, and life does not flow as smoothly as it could—and a lot of our projects, hopes, and dreams may be very difficult to reach and sometimes even fail.

Since the orders of love are subject to free will, when we choose to follow them it is an indication that we are connecting to a path of spiritual growth and that we are attracting to live from our hearts. When we do not follow these orders of love, we may be imprisoned in family entanglements through the "arrogant"/ "immature" love of our inner child.

By observing moral traditions of the Zulu culture, Hellinger has systematized the main orders of love in as follows (and there are other orders of love that stem from the three main ones): **precedence and hierarchy** (from which also comes the idea of "priority"); **the right to belong** (from which comes the healing energy of "inclusion"); and **balance in giving and receiving** (from which comes understanding of the "geometry" of vertical and horizontal relationships). These orders of love are stepping stones to the **CMLC**. They are the basis of all CM sessions and allow us to float in the benign currents of life.

Precedence and hierarchy mean that those who came first are bigger than those who came last. It is a generational hierarchy. This means that the oldest take care of the youngest and that is the order of life. Not only do they take care of them, they are responsible for them. Therefore, on a family energy field, grandparents are bigger than parents, parents are bigger than children, and so forth.

Concerning siblings, there is a small dose of that concerning who was born or who existed first. Firstborns have a little bit of hierarchy compared to younger siblings.

The right to belong means that when there is any type of exclusion in a system, especially a family system, there is a wound in the soul of the family. Exclusion means dishonoring the right to belong that we all hold as human beings. This may happen at a very unconscious level or it may be explicit to the conscious mind of some members of a generation.

Exclusion implies looking at the bigger picture of a **family system.** *This means all serious romantic relations,* pregnancies, hidden romances, and family secrets in general must be seen and acknowledged by the "formal" members. It means broadening the concept of legitimacy in the hearts of all family members, including everyone, and saying, "I see you. I respect you. You have a place in my heart."

The consequence of exclusion is that the next generations will be entangled with the drama or dishonor of excluded members. They might follow the footsteps of suffering of excluded members of generations past. If the soul of the family has contents or open wounds such as triangular relationships, dishonored lovers, parallel families, illicit money, hidden deaths, and secrets in general, these energies are resonating in the unconscious mind of all members, even if the conscious mind is not aware of it.

Once exclusion of an experience or person is highlighted, focused, and healed, by integrating the person or situation in the heart of a family member in a family constellation, everyone and everything is honored in his or her right to belong. That way, the wounds in the soul of the family begin to heal, and there is an alignment with the path for peace.

Balance in giving and receiving means that we need clarity about hierarchy for energy to flow in the right direction. In vertical relationships, which means from generation to generation, the oldest give and the youngest receive. This means that parents give and children receive.

Children can express their gratitude to their parents not by giving back to them, but by taking life and strength from them and doing something good with that life. We do something good with our lives when we move forward with it, create good things in the world, and share our gifts with humanity. This is how we thank our parents for the life that has been given to us.

When it comes to "horizontal relationships," the movement of life is different. Horizontal relationships are the connections we make with people from the same hierarchy/generation as ours—friends, lovers, husbands, wives, professional partners. We can't develop motherly, fatherly or childish behaviors with these people—it would become a "whirlpool" of stagnant energy instead of a balanced, healthy flow between people who love and admire each other.

In synthesis, concerning family systems, the orders of love express themselves in derivative principles such as priority (that comes from hierarchy and precedence), acknowledgement (that comes from the right to belong), and relationship roles (that come from balance in giving and receiving).

Family Soul Priorities
Priority means that kids come first. It is their turn now. Older people take care of children and not the contrary. When an adult person did not receive all the love and support he or she needed as a child, as a parent this person may "invert" the order of priority and emotionally behave as a child with his or her own children.

This makes the child confused because on a structural level, this child is small next to his or her parent. On a personality or behavioral level, the parent is not "reliable" as an adult. The parent behaves like a child and unconsciously "demands" their child the love he or she did not have from his or her own mother and father.

The child in turn gets very confused and suffers from the "inversion" in the flow of energy. Even as adults, if we have immature parents, we suffer emotional pain. This is one of the most common issues in **CMLC** and family constellation sessions.

Systemic Disorders: Individual Places and Obstacles to a Fulfilling Life

We are emotionally healthy within our families if we are aligned with the orders of love. If this aligned consciousness is balanced within us, we tend to be happy, healthy, emotionally and financially stable, and personally fulfilled. Schneider says that our lives get out of balance when we do not follow the natural and healthy orders of love because of family entanglements (Schneider, 2007).

We may be entangled in systemic issues because of our family history and because of our unconscious immature love of the inner child. As Jacob Schneider states, we may either be tied up in family entanglements, or living in the free flow of a good life. Family constellations and **CMLC** sessions bring liberation and relief to family entanglements, and for that we ask two questions: "what entangles people in the destinies of other people from the family past, and what is the liberating solution of love?"

Even if we are not aware of this, we are deeply connected to our ancestors, and this connection influences all our relationships, especially in giving and receiving. We may become compulsive in repeating painful situations because we are so connected and entangled.

The purpose of constellations and the **CMLC** is to heal and overcome wounds in the soul of the family—in our personal lives and in the lives of ancestors, especially if we are entangled because of what Hellinger calls the "immature love of the child."

This kind of love is well-intentioned but blind and ignorant of the orders of love that allow life to flow easily. With an intention to do good and with such intense compassion for the excluded and dishonored members of the family, the blind love of the child is unintendedly arrogant, delusional, and pretentiously "omnipotent." This love searches for subjective justice and compensation on a time in which there is nothing more to do about the traumas in the past of the family, and it only creates more useless pain and suffering in the present.

In this perspective, family souls hold what Schneider calls a "moral conscience" that evaluates its own behavior and acts from the principles of belonging, compensation, and order. Because of our blind love, these reference points may be out of balance in our individual lives.

In this perspective, there are three types of conscience that exist simultaneously in our psyches: **group consciousness** (which includes the family soul and the cultural soul), **individual consciousness** and **universal consciousness**. Whenever we are entangled in group consciousness behavior, we cannot develop into the next two levels of consciousness expansion, which are autonomous individual consciousness, and expanded universal consciousness, which is a feeling of belonging to humanity that goes beyond segregation, privilege or "selective affections" (Hume, 1875, 1985) that are typical of family psyches and cultural understandings.

In my **CMLC** experience, I've found that some of the most common unconscious behavior patterns described by Schneider are **representation**, when we are representing ancestors and excluded members by unconsciously following their life scripts; **urgency to help,** when we try to repair and satisfy older members who have been hurt in the past; **inversion**, when we are trying to take care of a parent's wounded inner child and occupying the place of a grandmother or grandfather on an emotional level (this can be visualized as if a leaf were trying to give the nutrients back to the trunk and root of a tree); **symbiosis**, when we are symbiotically connected to the painful experiences of parents, aunts, uncles, or ancestors; and **unanchored spirituality**, when we get into denial mode and "delete" the family past from our consciousness, disconnect ourselves from mother and father, and especially do not acknowledge parents as life givers and caretakers, engaging in an unanchored spiritual life.

The healing solutions that liberate us from these entanglements, in a **CMLC** perspective, are **alignment with your origins**, which means accepting and consenting to the precedence of each member of your family in the levels of hierarchy, and in the level of siblings (clarity in who is oldest and who is youngest); and **alignment with roles of men and women in the same generation**, especially when there is complex progression within families (mixed families, first husbands and first wives, divorces, second and third husbands and wives, children from the first marriage, children from the second marriage etc.).

Another solution is to establish **giving and receiving between parents and children in a continuous flow.** This means parents only give to children, and children only receive from parents. This cannot be stressed enough. Children thank their parents for the life they received from them by giving back to the world and not to their parents. Children pass on life to their own children and/or work for the good of society or humanity. Gratitude and respect for your parents will then manifest in a healthy and fruitful life for you.

On the level of free will and personal consciousness, it important to be in alignment with the integration of excluded members (once you get that clarity after a session) by seeing them and opening a place for them in your heart.

Grieving and allowing the dead to go is also very important, as well as giving farewell to your illusions, which means giving up on the omnipotence of magical thoughts of saving the "weak" and harmed. When you give up the savior complex, you give the weak and disadvantaged back their dignity. Giving up on fantasies of the inner child and facing the empty space that precedes emotional adulthood is a huge step into an expanded consciousness and a life-connection process.

Emotional reconciliation with excluded people that have caused pain in the family in your own life story, or in your parent's life, or in the life of an ancestor is also important. Acknowledge their existence and that they have a history with the family, as you give up on ideals of justice, guilt, and compensations. This is a great relief.

Overcoming trauma is also fundamental. We should let the past go. When we stop living in the past, we align ourselves with a clear mind and choose clarity over distorted emotions. When we make that decision, we are choosing mature love, which integrates all life experiences without energetic emotional charges, over the immature love of the reactive inner child.

Circles of Love and the Flow of Life
Bert Hellinger affirms that when you say yes to what is without resistance, everything that flows into our lives is strength (1999). This is when we consent to life as at is and abandon idealism.

Hellinger says that the journey of the human experience is a constant flow that moves us along through five levels of expanded consciousness. In his words, these levels of expanded consciousness are called "circles of love." These circles have distinct types of strength—from intense past bonds to new, expanded relationships. The first and second circles have the strongest influence in our archaic consciousness, our unconscious mind, and the family soul.

The First Circle
The first circle of love corresponds to everything that has happened in our family before we were born, including the moment our parents

met each other. We are deeply influenced by this past, and our archaic consciousness is strong on this level—particularly because it contains all the experiences of our parents and ancestors.

In a family constellations perspective, what determines this level is what has happened four generations back. In the **CMLC** perspective, we include seven generations back, following the broader references of Native American traditions. All people who have been hurt, excluded, dishonored, or harmed in the past of the family until the day our parents met each other belong to the first circle of love.

The Second Circle
This circle includes our gestational life, childhood, and teenage days. When we feel one with mother and father, as if we are part of them and being with them makes us feel whole, we are in the second circle of love. This does not have to be a pleasant feeling—it could be a very symbiotic and harsh relationship. Our parents do not have to be alive for this circle to be predominant in our lives either—emotionally, we may feel very connected and close to them. The point about the second circle is that if one of our parents, or both, are the gravitational center of our emotional lives, that is where we stand emotionally, and that is the place of a child or teenager, and not of the adult.

Our parents are indeed our biggest points of reference in life when we are children, but that starts to change when we are teenagers. When for some reason we get stuck in the second circle of love, though, we may become adults and still have that feeling. Again, this does not mean we have an easy relationship with them, because love is not as obvious as it may seem in sugarcoated fairytales.

This may express itself indirectly when we pick fights or try to call negative attention to ourselves with our parents. It is a distorted kind of love, but there is strong energy there. When our parents remain as our biggest points of reference and life literally revolves around them, we are emotionally stuck in the perspective of a young child. Many adults are stuck in this emotional level.

We can begin to get out of this circle when we start to realize that even if there were difficulties in our relationship with our parents, what is essential in that relationship is the life that has been given to us. If we are alive and reading this book, our life is strong and our integrity has remained intact. This is what matters for the functional consciousness of the soul, and we are alive because our parents made it happen.

When we realize and consent to the fact that life itself has not been harmed despite the difficulties we have had (which could be many, and by no means is there an intention here to invalidate emotional pain), a special kind of strength surfaces and gives us what Hellinger calls **depth of soul**. Even if we were hurt by one of our parents or both, understanding that life is larger and more powerful than any pain allows us to move on from the second circle and expand our lives to a new level of consciousness.

In this circle, we experience profound feelings of fulfillment within ourselves when we have a loving and grateful attitude toward our parents, and when we thank the love between them that resulted in our lives. We also feel thankful for all the people who have helped our parents in the process of having a child. This circle includes the ancestors behind our parents who have supported the life force within them in the process of giving birth and parenting. When we honor our parents in this circle, we are free to move forward in the continuous flow of life.

Since the second circle corresponds to childhood and puberty, when parents give all that they are and all that they have, and the children receive it, life can flow easily.

Some people may get confused in this circle, because what the parents are giving them is so great they feel they will never be able to reach that level of strength and start calculating ways to repay, reciprocate, or return it. Many people feel guilty about receiving too much form the parents, especially when the parents themselves or their ancestors may have received so little. This is a challenge to individual arrogance, but it happens on a very deep unconscious level.

Some children unconsciously feel guilty about having so much that they choose to take less from their parents, so they will not feel obliged to give back so much to life in return. And since the only resource children have is love, often in this circle they may choose to become "donors" and create a fantasy of taking emotional care of the parents. They may focus on the parents' childhood wounds and vulnerabilities, to repay them for all that they give, instead of looking forward and focusing on the abundant flow of life.

Surpassing the difficulties of this circle implies realizing that there is no need to give back to our parents directly. In fact, it is against the "orders of love" and the natural flow of life. Again, in the image of the **CMLC**, it would be like a leaf trying to give back the sap to the trunk or the roots. Hellinger says that adults can give back to the world what was given to them by doing something good for humanity and/or having children of their own.

Our challenge in the second circle is to observe and overcome our ability to include instead of excluding, to accept without complaining, to consent instead of judging. It is where something clicks inside of us and we choose to consent to all that has happened to our parents and ancestors without carrying any weight for them. When we do that without trying to solve the problems of those who are bigger than us, we make a choice to include all that is—and this attitude gives us strength to move from one level to the next.

Problems in the First and Second Circles

Obstacles to the flow of life in the first and second circles would be the following, in Schneider's description:

- Comforting and giving solace to parents who have lacked love from their own parents, meaning the child will move away from his or her place of birth in the family system and try to "substitute" the grandparents. To fulfill their place is to try to give our parents all the love they feel they lack from the original source. This inverted movement can especially be visualized in the work with the chakras in the **CMLC**, which will be explained in chapters 5 and 7 of this book.
- Partnerships between children and parents, which creates a hierarchy issue. This can be like what Freud described as Oedipus's or Electra's Complex, when the child steps in between the parents and tries to give mother or father or both what they believe the other parent has not given them as a loving partner, or even in understanding and friendship. It is a form of compensation. This constitutes an unconscious "triangle" in which the child disqualifies one of the parents or both and emotionally assumes the role of a partner in the parents' relationship.
- Interruption. When the small child is separated at a very early age from the biological mother or father or both, there is always emotional damage. Something has been interrupted, and this causes emotional shock. The movement of love that flows from the child is disrupted. The child feels abandoned, and even when the mother or father returns, the child cannot welcome the parent back with a loving, receptive attitude.
- Recrimination, which is when the child judges and censors one of the parents, or both, because of attitudes and personality traits. This attitude interrupts the free flow of love between parents and children.

- Depression is also a symptom of a person who does not know how to receive, and is only able to give. This is a distortion because giving makes us feel big and receiving makes us feel small, so it takes an allowing attitude of acceptance to balance the flow of giving and receiving. When we don't know how to receive, we are engaging in arrogance, not consenting to or accepting our parents as they are, and we are not embracing them in our hearts.
- Spirituality as an escape. According to Hellinger, spirituality brings great expansion of consciousness, if we include our family in our heart. If our spirituality excludes our parents, it may be escapism or denial, and our life will not be as pleasant as it could be. Specific types of spirituality, religions, and therapies separate adult children from their parents, which cuts away the flow of life from that person, because it excludes the functional level of consciousness in the archaic psyche of the family soul and disrespects the nature of the human condition. For some people, spirituality can be a very subtle and sophisticated way not to accept the parents.

Solutions to Problems in the First and Second Circles

When by our free will we consciously decide in our hearts to abandon the immature love of the child and connect to the love of the adult, we respect hierarchy by always saying please to our parents and ancestors when we ask for blessings in our lives. We recognize they are the source of life and abundance through which the higher energies of the universe manifest.

We say, "Thank you" to our parents for our lives, and through them, we thank all our ancestors. We say, "I am sorry" for all our arrogant behaviors. And we say, "Yes" to life and reality, which is a way to consent to what is. This is larger than accepting what is; it is about consenting. There is a difference between these two terms and it's important to be very mindful and aware of this.

The solutions to arrogance issues, be they conscious or unconscious, in the first and second circles are in understanding that our parents, both mother and father in equal proportion (and if a person is adopted, including the biological *and* the substitute parents), are the keys to life. This understanding manifests in these four attitudes: always saying "Please" and "Thank you" to parents and ancestors; apologizing to them for our arrogance, and saying "Yes" to what the present moment, life, and objective physical reality present to us, as they unfold in our everyday experience.

The Third Circle
The third circle of love corresponds to giving and taking and balance in giving and receiving in the same generation, which is different from giving and receiving between generations from different hierarchies. It is in the third circle that we take a partner and build our own family, when we get married and/or have children.

To Hellinger, unlike what we tend to think, it is much easier for the natural arrogance of our human condition to give than to take, because as it was said before, when we give we feel superior, and this reinforces our unconscious arrogance. We experience adulthood and mature love when we are equally able to give and take among equals in a continuous flow of moving life energy—especially in intimate relationships and marriage. This means, on a conscious level, that we take from the world and become equal like all others. It is in taking that we assume responsibility and become adults in the level of the soul.

In Hellinger's perspective, we can only give after we have taken life in order from our parents and the world. When we put ourselves in a position of taking, we admit to our needs, and that makes us equal in the human condition. It unites us to people. When we take something and value what we have taken, the soul evolves. Taking reciprocally may not necessarily be symmetric, but what is taken must be valued, all that is given must be valued, and there should be no demands in expecting something different or desiring to take what the other person cannot give.

And when we get married, build a business, have a child, thrive in the world, we are giving back to life the love that was given to us by our parents.

The Fourth and Fifth Circles
The first three circles correspond to the evolvement of personal consciousness from the level of family consciousness. Hellinger affirms that the fourth and fifth circles are beyond personal consciousness—they belong to the universal consciousness level. The fourth circle is a level of being that transcends individuality, in which we include all who belong to our families and social relationships in our hearts: those who were excluded, despised, or forgotten. We feel complete and fulfilled when we include them all.

The fifth circle expands this movement of inclusion to all humanity and to the world, when we feel love toward all people—even those we don't know, and among diverse cultures as well. The fifth circle is expressed in the feeling of universal love in the heart of a human being, and it might mean surrendering to superior powers and seeing each person in his or her own circumstances instead of passing judgment and engaging in exclusion. It is a spiritual conception of unconditional love.

This is a circle of indiscriminate and compassionate respect for all human beings, and through this attitude we grow into a higher spiritual level, which is different from the denser type of family love because, in Hellinger's words, primitive love does not understand much and may create stagnation in our souls if we do not surrender to Higher Consciousness and spiritual growth in the fourth and fifth circles—if we do not surrender to constant expansion in the flow of life.

Awareness of Self and Family Members

Family constellations are a very powerful modality that not only inspires, but works very well when combined with **CMLC** crystals. After we start working with crystals in a **CMLC** perspective, we will notice our insights and intuition are getting sharper on all levels of life, but especially concerning our families. Staying silent and not judging anybody as we just observe is the most powerful and healing attitude we can cultivate. We will in general become more aware of life, as freedom, love, peace, and joy bring us back to our natural state of being.

4

NATIVE AMERICAN WISDOMS

Alignment with the Outside World

Native American wisdoms are used in the **CMLC** as a reference to connect us to nature and how we position ourselves in the outside world. If we remember that for the **CMLC** everything is geometric, and what happens in the outside world is, in divine proportion, a reflection of our inner world, we can heal the contents of our minds with contact with nature and Native American wisdoms.

In many Native American cultures, stones and crystals are important instruments for healing the soul and spirit. In the **CMLC**, the most researched cultures are the Arawak, the Taino, the Aztecs, the Mayas, the Incas, the Mohawk, the Seneca, the Lakota, and the Hopi.

The most important Native American principles the **CMLC** uses are present in these cultures, especially mindfulness to maintain a balance in all our relationships, respecting individual boundaries, living from truth, and appropriate self-expression in all life cycles (childhood, youth, adulthood, mature life, and old age).

Mindfulness in all our relationships includes learning from one another, and constantly asking, "What do I have to learn from that person?" It also includes trying to live in harmony with all living creatures, healing ourselves and the Earth by listening to the signs and sounds of nature, and expressing our own unique individual talents. This is all part of a fulfilling life and is considered in a **CMLC** perspective as life-connection practices.

In the vision of these Native American wisdoms, the calmest waters seem to run in the depths, and connecting to the depths requires silence. Depth of soul and self-connection allow us to hear and understand the sounds and to see the signs of nature. In silence, we become one with the universe, meaning we will heal whatever needs to be healed when we feel integrated with all beings.

According to many cultures in Native American wisdoms, healing of body, mind, and spirit comes from sources such as connecting to nature, which means two things: living close to nature and connecting to it, and expressing our own nature freely. Natural living requires contact with nature, so that we can recognize and express our unique talents. Recognizing and expressing our unique talents is part of natural living in these cultures.

Following these two principles of natural living leads us to a life in the path of "Hail-lo-way-ain," which in the Seneca language means "the language of love." Love in this perspective is an expression of respectful and harmonious relationships in which everyone speaks the truth. Love is not about lying to avoid emotional pain or people pleasing. On the contrary, it involves compassion, which is different from empathy, and mutual respect. These two forces complement each other.

What Jamie Sams (Sams, 1998) calls "The Path of Wisdom" is living in constant retribution of love to the Great Mystery. It means surrendering to a benign current of life without aiming to control anything. Surrendering to the Great Mystery is the most powerful healing process possible on any level of existence: body, mind, emotions, or spirit, and in the **CMLC** perspective, surrendering to the movements and the past of the family soul instead of reacting to it.

This means seeing that each human being we get in touch with is a master and a friend, no matter the circumstances. When we understand this deep wisdom, it brings unity to the heart and makes us whole and one with all creatures of nature. The basic human value must then be, in Sam's vision, to recognize the existence of a unified world in which we are all one. From this standpoint, all humanity has the same origin and goes through the same challenges in various levels of consciousness. Some human beings go through life experiences in reaction mode; others contemplate the lesson and choose love.

In the Native American cultures Sams describes, the sun and the moon are our grandparents, the sky is father to us all, the Earth is our mother, and stones, plants, animals, and humans are all on the same level, or hierarchy, of creation. The Path of Wisdom is to "restore connection" with all living beings and understand their levels of being, coexisting in harmony and integration.

Being in the world is an orderly experience if we connect to nature and the forces of nature. One of the ways to understand and organize our life experience is to know the cardinal points and the cardinal directions. Native American wisdoms have different perspectives that vary from culture to culture, and the **CMLC** has chosen a few of these references to use as practical tools for life connection.

In its current state of art, the basic **Cardinal Method of Life Connection** Native-American references are the South American *Chakana* and the North American medicine wheel.

The Chakana is an Andean traditional native image that transcends that encompasses many symbols. There are eight two-dimensional geographic directions superimposed on a square and there is also a circle in the middle. The Chakana symbol had social organizational purposes and deep spiritual meaning, since Andean cultures did not fathom the difference between the material world and the spiritual world, nor did they have any concept of good or bad. There was a clear image of higher and lower realms but that did not mean they were superior or inferior to one another.

The Chakana image transcends the dualistic mind and promotes integration between the world within and the external world (Calverley, 2013). It is not only a symbol of transcendence from the material world, but also of integration between the spiritual and the material, in which the material may manifest spiritual perfection.

In the **CMLC**, the symmetric geometry of the Chakana is an inspiration to balance all levels of our lives. When our energy is distributed in a symmetric and balanced way, we find peace of mind and become autonomous, healthy, productive human beings. This is part of the spiritual wisdom of Andean cultures (Torra, 2014) incorporated in the **CMLC**.

The hole in the middle "symbolizes the clear, empty mind of bare awareness" (Calverley, 2013), and achieving this state in the form of insights with the crystal practices is one of the purposes of the **CMLC**.

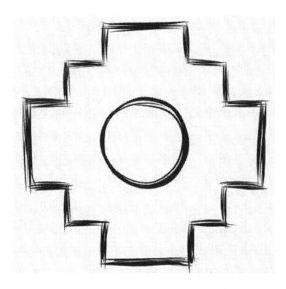

The North American medicine wheel is considered a sacred ceremonial space where the beauty of life in the physical world is experienced. This is called life connection in a **CMLC** perspective. The medicine wheel is built on the ground with stones and represents movement, changes, and cycles in our physical world.

The medicine wheel has twelve two-dimensional directions like the hours of a clock, and three sacred directions that are three-dimensional: above, below, and within. The four main cardinal directions (north, south, east, and west) follow a circular path in a counterclockwise movement that symbolizes the path of human experience: east, south, west, and north.

In a spiritual wisdom perspective, author Jamie Sams says each cardinal direction has different energy pathways that nourish our lives in very specific ways (Sams, 1990, 1998). They correspond to different challenges in our life cycles and the human journey. The idea in the **CMLC** is to understand these cycles and go beyond them, living in a state of bliss that surpasses duality and embraces the cycles of life with more consciousness and awareness of its natural movements.

Also, the portals of the medicine wheel bring powers, talents, and lessons as immediate answers to our life challenges that come through the wind (Sams, 1990), and this is present in **CMLC** practices by the speed and flow of accurate information that comes through crystals.

The wheel includes twelve points (like the twelve hours of the clock), and the four main ones are east, south, west and north. Connecting east to west is a line called the Blue Spirit Road, and connecting south to north is the Good Red Road of physical existence.

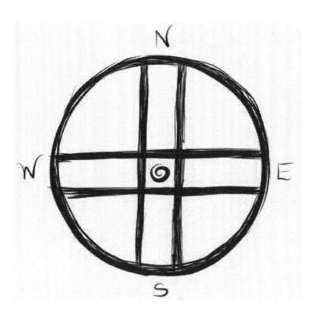

The four main cardinal directions are considered "gates" or portals to spiritual realities that bring different gifts to humanity. The colors and the animals associated with these directions vary according to different Native American cultures, and in the **CMLC** the references are mostly Cherokee and Seneca, following the work of Jamie Sams, (1990, 1998):

- The east is where the sun rises and represents birth and rebirth, bringing the gifts of the eagle, especially common sense and logical ideas.
- Following a counterclockwise movement, the south is the place of our childhood, bringing the gifts of the coyote, which heals the inner child and comes with laughter and humility.
- The west is the place of adulthood, bringing the gifts of the bear with conscious choices of free will, self-connection, withdrawal from the external world, courage, and intuition.
- The north is the place of the elders, bringing the gifts of the buffalo, which are silence and wisdom.

In a **CMLC** perspective, the directions bring especially the following gifts:

- **East**: healing (science, medicine, and logical thinking), creative talents (art), balance in giving and receiving (healthy relationships with money and exchanges, economy)
- **South**: health of the physical body, spontaneous laughter, authenticity, pleasure of being alive, nonjudgment of self and others, healthy inner child, understanding that all relationships are mirrors of some aspect of self
- **West**: mature love, responsibility, adult choices, healing of the ego with deep love
- **North**: gratitude for life, prayer, wisdom, silence, spiritual life

Between the each of the four main directions there are two middle directions in the medicine wheel, and in the middle, are the three-dimensional directions, called "sacred directions," which are above, below, and within.

When we embrace these gifts, "Life becomes extraordinary, exciting, and filled with beauty. The mundane awareness of daily living melts away when we pause to sense the adventure offered by the constant messages brought by the Four Winds of Change. Everywhere we look, life is calling" (Sams, 1990).

This is what the **CMLC** calls **languages of consciousness**, and when we think of the two paths in medicine wheel, which are the Blue Path and the Red Path, it makes even more sense. The Blue Path is exclusively spiritual, and it is where the spirits who are not incarnated continue their journey. The Red Path, or "Good Red Road", is the path of a human life, in which we integrate physical existence and spirituality. When spiritual meaning permeates a human life, our hearts are filled with peace, wisdom, and joy as we travel "The Good Red Road".

In the **CMLC**, we superimpose two very strong symbols of North American Native cultural imagery described by Jamie Sams: The medicine wheel and the symbol of the arrow.

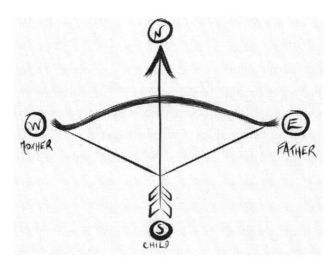

The Symbol of the Arrow in Native American Wisdoms
"The Arrow is straight and true, weighing all future possibilities" (Sams, 1990). It is a symbol of protection in Native American wisdom, but on a soul level it is symbolic of courage and of truth. The value of the arrow includes being stable and compassionate and the wisdom of staying in silence for prolonged periods of time listening to elders who came before.

It takes courage to live from the heart, but in Jamie Sams's words, there needs to be a balance between truth, common sense, physical excellence, integrity, and connection to spirit (Sams, 1990).

The arrow is shot and has a straight and true movement when released through the "Bow of Beauty": "The Bow of Beauty is the arch of inner strength that gave flight to the Arrow. It was said to be made of the finest gold, which represented the Golden Light of Grandfather Sun's love, and was inlaid with pearls, which represented the essence of Grandmother Moon's nurturing. At the core is the balanced male/female of each Brave. The balance was found through the willingness to bend like the bow of Beauty and send the Arrow of truth into the world" (Sams, 1990).

In a **CMLC** perspective, we are the arrow, and our parents and ancestors are the Bow of Life, which corresponds to the "Bow of Beauty" in Native American wisdom We take the strength from the father from the east (the place of enlightenment) and from the mother from the west (the place of love). In the middle, we place ourselves as the arrow and shoot, straight and true, from the south to the north in the direction of our mission and life purpose.

The **CMLC** arrow points to the light within and gives life meaning, as Tarso Firace explains in his work that integrates family constellations and consciousness expansion in a quantum physics framework (2014). There will be further explanation about Firace's work in chapter 6 of this book.

Healing Archetypal Pain with the Symbol of the Arrow in Western Cultures

One specific **CMLC** session, called the "Arrow Session," is inspired in healing individual and family emotional pain by the archetypal symbol of the arrow.

The symbol of the arrow is used as an archetypical image in many cultures, as a mystical or philosophical reference, such as in Greek mythology (Artemis, Apollo, and Chiron), the Enneagram, the arrow symbol in crystallography, the book *Zen and the Art of Archery* (Herrigel, 1999), the idea of an astrological north node, the idea of truth in Native American wisdoms, and many others.

In The **Cardinal Method of Life Connection**, the arrow is used as a symbol to point to and encourage the best path, or the path of our divine nature or virtuous core. In a family constellations perspective, this means honoring and taking the strength from the mother and father (and all ancestors on both sides). Combined with Native American wisdoms, the **CMLC** considers the bow as the parents and the individual as the arrow, going straight to the target of his or her sacred path. If we take the strength from both parents in a balanced way and let ourselves follow the "sacred path" of our individual lives in a clear and aligned direction toward our target, we connect to love, abundance, health, and well-being.

As we look at some of the myths and symbols that inspire this session, we can get a deeper and clearer vision of how the Arrow Session works. In Greek mythology, the archetypal gods express the dualistic nature of the human life. In the **CMLC**, our focus is to integrate the dualistic understanding into a unified perspective as we heal emotional wounds and painful programming from the past with crystals. The crystals align and harmonize these archetypal energies so they express the possibilities of strength, love, and joy, and not the distortions and destructive aspects.

The Myth of Artemis and Apollo
This myth is important for the **CMLC** because it expresses all three principles of family constellations (hierarchy, the right to belong, and balance in giving and receiving). It also expresses some of the possible compensation mechanisms that were discussed before when these principles are violated.

In general terms, in this myth Leto, a child of Titans of godly nature, became pregnant from Zeus with the twins Artemis and Apollo, before Zeus was married to Hera. Hera was angry and jealous about the fact that her husband to be had gotten another woman pregnant, and she was so jealous and angry that she sabotaged Leto in many ways, forbidding gods and humans to help her with the delivery of the twin gods. Leto went through many difficulties and challenging times with the birth of her children since no one would help her, and finally gave birth to two powerful children, a girl born first (Artemis) and a boy born second (Apollo), representing the strength of pure female energy and the strength of pure masculine energy archetypes.

Artemis is the goddess of the moon, hunt, wilderness, and childbirth, the protector of girl children until they got married, and the holder of silver bows and arrows. In a **CMLC** perspective, the most important aspect of Artemis's strength is connection to nature and the natural world.

Apollo is the god of the sun, music, poetry, medicine, and healing, and of the truth expressed in oracles and prophecies. He was also the protector of boys until they reached adulthood, and the holder of a golden lyre, a golden chariot that moved the sun, and a bow with arrows made of gold.

In the **CMLC** perspective, the archetype of Apollo is more connected to the idea of a life purpose and a sacred path rather than rigid and immutable possibilities of destiny. The most important aspects of Artemis's attributes are our connection to the truth and our life purpose. In Greek mythology, it was said that Apollo was a god that healed but that could also bring plague and disease, and in the **CMLC** perspective, this symbolizes not only that when we live in the truth we are more resilient to these problems, but also that, as the god of the sun, the light of the sun also symbolizes clarity and the truth.

The relationship among Zeus, Leto, and Hera shows the almost universal problem of triangular connections in love relationships and the fact that many humans struggle with "polyamorous" internal worlds, which means a person may have feelings of romantic love with more than one person, and not exclusive love for one specific significant other.

Artemis and Apollo, the offspring of this story, on the level of duality seem to be representing a compensation for the vulnerability of falling in love and affirming individual powers and strength and very independent and autonomous versions of pure feminine and masculine energy. On a synthesis level, however, when balanced, they can coexist with other aspects of the psyche in a healthy way, connecting us to nature and to truth and keeping our feminine and masculine arrows pointed to the target of our life purpose, on the tracks of our sacred paths.

The Myth of Chiron
The **CMLC** incorporates another important Greek mythology archetype that is implicit in the symbol of the arrow: the myth of Chiron (Greene, 2000). Chiron was one of the sons of Chronos, the god of time in Greek mythology. He was a kind, wise creature and the king of the centaurs, a race that was half animal (horse) and half human. The centaurs were in general bestial and aggressive half the time, expressing the duality of human nature in which we engage in destruction, bestial behavior, and war—even if only in our minds.

Chiron, however, had a divine origin, so his divine aspect made him a wise, compassionate presence on Earth. With his threefold nature—half of an animal body, half of a human body, and a divine hear—he was well respected and trusted by all. Human kings would send their children to be educated by him both in physical and moral abilities, and Chiron was a mentor to many.

When he was trying to pacify a battle between centaurs and a giant friend of his, a poisoned arrow accidently wounded Chiron. Since he had divine immortality as the son of one of the gods, he had to deal with the pain without ever dying. On a symbolic level, the poisoned arrow can be associated with our toxic thoughts and toxic minds (Greene, 2000). In the history of the human condition in Western culture, toxic thoughts and toxic emotions poison our lives, steal our peace and unity, and only seem to be released in death.

The myth of Chiron is important for the **CMLC** because this release of the poison arrow can happen in our human lives when the dualistic, controlling mind gives in to the unified, integrated Higher Self aspect of our psyches. It seems like humanity is ready for this quantum leap in consciousness expansion, and the **CMLC** Arrow Session was designed for that purpose.

In a **CMLC** perspective, the archetypes of Artemis and Apollo help heal the wounded inner child with the contemplation of beauty through nature (Artemis) and art (Apollo), as they both serve as examples of feminine and masculine emotional independence.

The myth of Chiron is used to help heal the ego and allow it to surrender to the strength of an immortal spiritual life, in which there is no duality (abandoning the short circuits that may occur between animal instincts and desires and human needs), as wisdom encourages the ego to surrender, and the Higher Self and our divine nature begin to rule our lives. When the Higher Self starts to take over, the idea of a life purpose with deeper meaning becomes more relevant. This is when the idea of an astrological north node can be useful to transcend the duality of the human condition and become a point of reference and a spiritual portal to unity and divine living.

Our Lives' Purpose and the North Node
The north node is an astrological concept, and in astrology it points to our life purpose and to which behavior pattern we should adopt, and which autopilot behaviors should be released. The **CMLC** is not an oracle, nor does it embrace many of the tendencies of astrology to observe and predict the future. Astrology also expresses the dualistic aspect of human nature in the astrological signs and conceptions of the planets and houses, which is not something the **CMLC** does.

What is considered in the **CMLC** is the idea of a life purpose in astrological charts expressed by the north node (Spiller, 1997). The

CMLC focuses solely on the nature of the astrological signs as archetypes, how we can choose to live from their benign aspects, and how we can stop fueling the destructive ones. The Arrow Session also points to the virtuous core of our nature and to the benign current of our north node as well.

The Enneagram

The Enneagram is an important indirect influence for the **CMLC** and serves as inspiration especially because of the idea of arrows pointing to the direction of a fulfilling, meaningful life of love, peace, truth, and joy. This book will not dive into the depth of details of this powerful system, but the general idea that there is an upward spiral and a downward spiral, and that we have internal radars to guide our path, is important.

The Enneagram is a very ancient symbol of the human experience. The general theory of the Enneagram is important for the **CMLC** because it describes emotional distortions and limiting belief systems that crystalize in specific types of personalities, which can range from unhealthy, through medium, to healthy (Riso and Hudson, 1999; Palmer, 1991). The image of the Enneagram uses arrows and incorporates healthy and unhealthy movements of the psyche.

There are nine ways to "miss the target" in the Enneagram perspective. We miss the target when we deviate from virtues and engage in actions that are opposite to virtuous behavior. The more we act on the deviation, the more we crystallize emotional and mental structures that block the expression of our virtuous core and create a distorted sense of self. These nine "places" in the Enneagram wheel can be compared to the seven sins in Christianity but are much more ancient. The points have numbers, and the arrows in the image below point to the virtuous path, in which we can make movements toward personal growth.

According to this knowledge, in childhood we are wounded in one of these nine virtuous places of the psyche and develop personality defenses that are the opposite of these virtues. For example, if our childhood wound relates to fear, we become fearful of life. We feel all the emotions, but one of the nine is especially crystallized in our personality.

Point one relates to the virtue of serenity and is disrupted by anger/wrath on the emotional level, and perfectionism on a mental level. When expressing the destructive vibrations of this place in the psyche, these people who have developed a type-one personality tend to be perfectionists and/or angry.

Point two relates to the virtue of humility, which is disrupted by pride/arrogance on the emotional level, and these people develop flattery as a strategy of social survival on the mental level. These people tend to think they do not need any help or care when they are expressing the destructive vibrations of this place in the psyche, and that they are an infinite well of love and compassion to others, which makes them compulsive givers.

Point three relates to the virtue of authenticity and when disrupted creates vanity and self-centeredness on the emotional level, and illusions about the self on the mental level. When expressing the destructive vibrations of this place in the psyche, type-three people tend to become overachievers and workaholics with no real time for emotional connection with self or others.

Point four relates to the virtue of equanimity and internal balance. When disrupted, this place in the psyche creates melodramatic personalities and envy of others on the emotional level, and comparison and competition of the mental level. Type-four people become victims of the world and hypochondriacs when expressing the destructive vibrations of this place in the psyche.

Point five refers to the virtue of detachment and when disrupted creates avarice and isolation on the emotional level, and the strategy of disqualification on the mental level. Type-five people who express the destructive vibrations of this place in the psyche become eccentric loners who have very little contact with other people and the world, often frustrated for not fulfilling all their potentials.

Point six refers to the virtues of courage and faith and when disrupted creates fear of life on the emotional level, and the rationalization of the world on a mental level. Type-six people who express the destructive vibrations of this space in the psyche become paranoid and dependent, thinking they cannot survive on their own.

Point seven refers to the virtue of sobriety, and when disrupted creates compulsive behavior and gluttony on the emotional level, and the strategy of charlatanism on the mental level. Type-seven people become reckless and irresponsible when expressing the destructive vibrations of this place in the psyche.

Point eight refers to the virtue of innocence, and when disrupted creates intensity, associated with oppressive and authoritarian behavior on the emotional level, and the strategy of command on the mental level. Type-eight people become oppressive and intense when expressing the destructive vibrations of this place in the psyche.

Point nine refers to the virtue of essential inspired action and when disrupted creates abandonment of self and lethargy on the emotional level, and mechanical, autopilot living on the mental level, which means the person occupies himself or herself with trivial activities to avoid self-connection. When living from the destructive vibrations of this place in the psyche, these people become self-indulgent and lazy with their own dreams and potentials.

When we understand where we stand in the Enneagram (and this requires dedication and commitment to the Enneagram system—it will not happen just by reading these brief descriptions or even books about it), we can also see where we can find the path to healing and spiritual growth in the most important virtues to cultivate.

The **CMLC** uses the symbol of the arrow to point in the direction of the Higher Self, and though this is not the same idea as the Enneagram symbol, such as the Enneagram purpose of self-understanding, consciousness development, and personal growth, the **CMLC** is also about "pointing to" our virtuous core and "hitting the target" of peace of mind, self-connection, and life purpose. In a **CMLC** perspective, the emotional distortions tend to come mostly from inner-child wounds, and the limiting belief systems come from the ego.

The specific Enneagram types, which are nine, will not discussed in this book and have not yet even been brought up in **CMLC** sessions, but the types can be very nurturing and valuable knowledge in a self-connection discovery and a life-connection journey.

In a spiritual approach to the Enneagram, the idea of "sin" is when we miss the target of our virtues. The arrows in the Enneagram image are either pointed toward spiritual growth or degeneration. When we act form the Higher Self, or when our psyches are closer to the Higher Self, we are in an integration movement, and life flows in creative, joyful, and harmonious currents. When we are in a state of disconnection with the Higher Self, we tend to be in stagnation or, even worse, in a downward spiral of self-sabotaging behavior that in the unhealthier levels may lead to self-destruction.

Type-one people must cultivate the virtue of sobriety in point seven to dissolve anger and perfectionism. Type-two people must cultivate the virtue of equanimity in point four to dissolve pride.

Type-three people must cultivate the virtue of courage and faith, focusing on humanity and not the self, to dissolve vanity. Type-four people must cultivate the virtue of serenity in point one to dissolve envy and comparison to others. Type-five people must cultivate the virtue of innocence and spontaneous actions in point eight to dissolve isolation and avarice. Type-six people must cultivate the virtue of essential, inspired action and autonomy in point nine and to dissolve dependency and fear. Type-seven people must cultivate the virtue of detachment and frugality in point five to dissolve compulsiveness and gluttony. Type-eight people must cultivate the virtue of humility in point two to dissolve egocentrism. Type-nine people must cultivate the virtue of authenticity in point three to connect to self and dissolve self-abandonment.

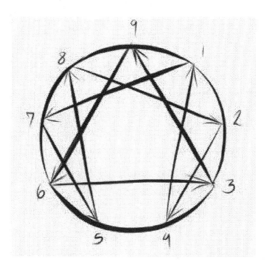

The virtues are in each of the nine places of the psyche in the Enneagram image and serve as inspirational movements. For the **CMLC**, these places of inspiration are in the images of the arrows and the movements of integration toward personal and spiritual growth. When we follow a virtuous path of personal growth, life flows. When we engage in stagnation and self-sabotaging behavior, we follow a destructive path. Personal growth and spiritual virtues are key factors to engage in the mature love of the adult, or the "age of reason," instead of living from family loyalty or past ancestral or parental pain.

There are many theories within the Enneagram expert community, and research and exploring are always recommended, but the idea in the **CMLC** is to understand that this inspiration uses the symbol of the arrow to point the way toward either integration or the downward spiral, and that the **CMLC** uses the symbol of the arrow to point to the direction of the Higher Self and to the fulfillment of our life purpose.

Symmetry, Mirrors, and Arrows in the CMLC
The idea of symmetry is very important to modern physics, and the intention here is not to engage in specific scientific terms, but only to observe that symmetry relates to invariance of features in a system and that this can be used for consciousness expansion and soul-healing purposes.

Arrows can point in the direction of deterioration and destruction, or in the direction of growth and expansion. When we observe this in a **CMLC** perspective, considering both family souls and the individual human mind and how the outside world presents these contents to us, the principles of symmetry, plug-and-socket mechanisms, or "it takes two to tango" may be elucidative.

In simple terms, the outside world is a mirror image of our internal world. We are never victims of the circumstances, but rather, we are living experiences that we are attracting consciously or unconsciously. These experiences may be tough or mild, but they are symmetric in nature to the contents of our conscious or unconscious minds.

When we let this knowledge sink in, we begin to live in beauty, because we realize we are cocreators of our lives in partnerships between the mind and the inner child, ego, or Higher Self. When we work with crystals and Native American wisdoms, our minds pair up with our Higher Selves.

The Arrow in a Cardinal Method of Life Connection
The **CMLC** arrow that we create with crystals in individual sessions incorporates all the symbols and archetypes described above. It is originally designed to point to a solution, and the solution is always a movement of energy toward consciousness expansion.

5

THE HINDU CHAKRAS SYSTEM

Individual Consciousness Alignment

For the **CMLC**, the Hindu chakras system is a very important reference of individual connection with higher realms and awakening our connection with God within and aligning in a vertical line with God Most High.

The Hindu chakras system is also compatible with the idea of living according to a moral compass within us, as Kant would say; developing objective and logical thinking, which eliminates distortions, subjective thinking, and filters of the mind; and aligning the whole body to promote unity on all levels.

This system is also an inspiration to work on the inner world and to know ourselves. For this reason, I encourage you to start connecting to the chakras on a practical level by coloring the images I created and illustrated in this chapter. I suggest you use the colors and tones I describe, and as you color, focus on your intentions to release the distortions that reside in each chakra. This is a subtle way to start looking within and to create a life connection.

As we explore and clear our inner world, we take responsibility for our lives and contribute to humanity, because a peaceful world within creates a peaceful world outside of us. The root of all problems and the source of all solutions are in our hearts.

There is an ancient Hindu proverb that says:

> If the heart is pure, there is beauty of character;
> If there is beauty of character, there is harmony at home;
> If there is harmony at home, there is order in the Nation;
> If there is order in the Nation, there is peace on Earth.

Hindu Knowledge

There are several types of chakra systems in diverse cultures. Tibetan and Native American traditions work with a five-chakras model, in which they are displayed in five chakras as a moving energy configuration (Tibetan) or vertically aligned (Native American, in which the solar plexus is a representation of the third lower chakras and the material world).

The Hindu chakras system has an older version in the yoga sutras of Patanjali, in which they are energy centers located in the body, but they have no specific colors, and later in the eighth century AD with the *Mahanirvana Tantra*, which gives the Hindu chakras a much more complex structure, including colors, deities, seminal syllables, sacred sounds, and emotional attributes.

The Yogasutras of Patanjali

As Carlos Eduardo Barbosa would comment in his translation of the *Yogasutras* of Patanjali,

> the correct practice of yoga allows our body intelligence to emerge in our minds, transforming our material lives in a metaphor of our own creations and the ways of the Universe. When we align ourselves with the unity of our body intelligence and the ways of the

universe, our minds are free from the possibility of error, pain, and impermanence. The illumination of our conscience by the practice of yoga brings us closer to our spiritual source and makes us feel perfectly integrated with God, Humanity, and all forces of Nature. (Patanjali, C. E. B, 1999).

The *Yogasutras* suggest that when we connect consciousness to the physical body, we engage in consciousness expansion, because the flow of energy is activated and we no longer feel imprisoned in a universe of physical matter. This is an important concept for the **CMLC**.

Chakras

A chakra is a place or energetic space in which vital, nourishing energy flows through us. In a **CMLC** perspective, when crystals are used on the chakras, they eliminate distortions, because their internal geometry acts on the subtle and energetic levels of the chakras, aligning consciousness and mind with higher vibrations.

As vortexes of energy in the body, chakras transmute energy into matter and matter into energy. In Hindu culture, chakras are described without much detail in the *Yogasutras* of Patanjali, and later with much more detail in the *Mahanirvana Tantra* (Johari, 2000). In this more recent Hindu tradition, there are other chakras above and below the head and pelvis, but seven of them are considered primary centers connected by an energy channel that runs through the spine. Two of these chakras are vertical (Crown and Root) and five are horizontal. Each horizontal chakra expresses itself as a funnel in front and a funnel in the back.

Nadis

Mahanirvana Tantra describes not only chakras, but also energy channels in the body called *nadis*, which mean "streams" in Sanskrit. The nadis are subtle energy currents through which life flows. According to this knowledge, there are 108 nadis in the body, and *Ida*, *Pingala*, and *Sushumna* are the central ones.

Ida is the left channel. It originates on the left side of the root chakra and ends in our left nostril. It governs the left eye and expresses the feminine energy of the moon. Ida has a magnetic, visual, and emotional nature, symbolizing the receptive aspects of our being. In the **CMLC**, Ida corresponds to the energy of our mother.

Pingala is the right channel. It originates on the right side of the root chakra and ends in our right nostril. It governs the right eye and expresses masculine solar energy. Pingala has a muscular, mental, and fiery nature, and is related to the active, self-affirming aspects of our being. In the **CMLC**, Pingala corresponds to the energy of our father.

Sushumna is the vertical central channel and is considered the most important nadi in the body. In the **CMLC**, it is associated with the self. Sushumna runs through the spine. It originates in the root chakra and goes through the palate until it reaches the crown chakra on the top of the head. According to tantric scriptures, the Sushumna channel is composed of three internal layers that also correspond to a masculine nature, a feminine nature, and a "synthesis" nature of cosmic consciousness.

The seven central chakras in the physical body are connected by the Sushumna channel. In Hindu tradition, these three major energy channels in the body, Ida, Pingala, and Sushumna (Johari, 2000) correspond to masculine and feminine energy and intertwine like DNA strands from the root chakra to the throat chakra until they reach our nostrils. Sushumna is vertical and straight and stands as a symmetrical reference of integration in the middle of these two polarized channels.

THE CARDINAL METHOD OF LIFE CONNECTION

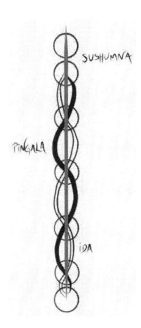

The chakras are nurtured by the nadis, and their main function is to absorb, metabolize, and expand the energy of the universe. Each chakra metabolizes specific energy and has specific consciousness functions.

The chakras also detect information about the world around us. Many sources of literature will say that a balanced chakra will spin clockwise and expands in spiral shape, keeping us focused and connected to the vital center of energy that flows within the body and connected to the Supreme Life Force. This literature will also say that when a chakra rotates counterclockwise, the vital energy moves from the dorsal center and emanates out of the body. We can also recoil distortions that emanate from the chakras in a counterclockwise movement, according to the *Yogasutras* of Patanjali.

Chakras are unhealthy when they are when there is no energy movement, which brings stagnation and blocks the chakra. Blocked chakras confuse our metabolism on a physical level and prevent proper absorption of world information on a subtle level. When a chakra is blocked or stagnant, our perception of the world changes, and we see through distorted filters and do not absorb the precise information.

If the chakras revolve counterclockwise, rather than absorbing the energies of the universe, they project our individual energy out. This confuses the objectivity of our minds, and we begin to feel as if reality is what our internal world emanates—a phenomenon otherwise known as projection.

When we feel as if our individual subjectivity is the reality of the world, the Hindu tradition calls this phenomenon *vittris* (Johari, 2000). We project our imaginary internal realities into the external world and see it through our distortions. With this distorted way of seeing life, we interpret the present moment and the unfolding of life as if everything was a repetition of the images that have been formed in our minds through our individual experiences. This seems especially true regarding our childhood memories.

Closely related to the individual experience of each person, these subjective projections, or *vittris*, are very particular because each experience is personal, unique, and nontransferable, bringing us back once again to the subjective inner worlds described by Thomas Hobbes.

The projections through chakras come from the specific area of location of each one of them, and these areas have specific types of consciousness. Since chakras are interconnected, what affects one chakra will eventually travel through the channel of connection and affect the next one, either positively or negatively. According to Johari, since our modern human experience is so disconnected from our life source and people rarely meditate, most human beings tend to have three or four chakras blocked at some point (Johari, 2000). For the sake of consciousness expansion, it is necessary to constantly clear, balance, and strengthen our chakras to improve the overall condition of our bodies to strengthen our physical, emotional, mental, and spiritual health.

The arrangement of seven major chakras following a vertical line along the spine with a chromatic scale are described in detail by *Mahanirvana Tantra,* and the connections between the chakras form a path. The pure energy conducted through this path was chosen as one of the references in **The Cardinal Method of Life Connection** that represents the individual path of each one of us. Since the chakras relate to physical health, to emotional and psychological balance, and to higher levels of spiritual consciousness, this is a complete system of life connection on its own.

In some contemporary views of energy medicine, there are seven main chakras described in *Mahanirvana Tantra,* and other minor chakras anchored in the physical body. In the **CMLC** we mainly observe the seven chakras along the spine and skull: *Muladhara* (root chakra, first chakra anchored in our physical body), *Swadhisthana* (sexual or sacral chakra), *Manipura* (solar plexus or spleen chakra), *Anahata* (heart chakra), *Vishuddha* (throat chakra), *Ajna* (brow or third-eye chakra), and *Sahashara* (crown chakra, the last one anchored in the physical body).

Chakras are described as vortexes, but the image of a lotus flower to symbolize them is also used in the more poetic version of the *Mahanirvana Tantra.* Each chakra has a different number of petals, which the *Mahanirvana Tantra* describes as mind challenges we need to conquer with spiritual strength.

In the **CMLC**, despite the vast array of detailed information regarding animals, deities, and sounds, the "petals" are the most important focus as centers for consciousness and awareness. These "petals" refer to the most important mental modifications (Johari, 2000) or belief systems that rule our emotions, and eventually our physiology

(Veltheim, 2011). When we observe the consciousness level of these "petals," we can unblock our minds and release limiting beliefs—if we have the necessary discipline.

These seven major chakras are anchored in the human body and are represented in Hindu culture by images of lotus flowers with different numbers of petals, besides their animals, sounds, mantras, a divine couple (a male deity and its corresponding female consort to each main chakra), and other aspects. These petals represent specific qualities that are to be overcome, balanced, or cultivated, depending on the chakra in question. More than just qualities, the petals indicate trends or automatic movements inherent in the human condition, which will be detailed further along in this book.

The focus of the **CMLC**, is therefore in the colors (which are considered an important language of the soul) and the indication of specific types of emotions, ideas, or energies of the petals.

The effort to balance all the attributes of the chakras depends on each person's free will. The choices and deliveries of each of us, the self-discipline, and the courage to admit our own failures and to deepen self-knowledge is a very personal journey. Various spiritual traditions affirm that when we make a choice, we can disrupt our lives, and when we surrender to the "right path," it unfolds immediately in a calm, firm, and free-of-doubt manner. In this perspective of giving up free will on behalf of the surrender to a more powerful, benign life force, the path to take is not presented as a mental prison in an obsessive way, but rather, we become less vulnerable to the frivolous temptations of having too many options and losing focus.

Surrender and delivery of the right path come from within. It is a feeling that there is only one best road, only one way of living that always and consistently makes sense to us. This benign flow presents itself to us when all seven main chakras are aligned and properly connected.

Following the proper course of this journey leads to a lifetime that many Native American wisdoms call "The Sacred Path," or in this physical life, it is the "Good Red Road," or what the **CMLC** calls "the aligned pathway."

Knowing the basic characteristics of the seven main chakras is important for consciousness expansion and for some knowledge about how distinct types of consciousness manifest in the physical body. In a **CMLC** perspective, everything happens on the subtle, conscious, and energetic levels before they manifest in our lives and physical bodies. Below are some general descriptions of the most relevant aspects of each main chakra.

Muladhara—the Base or Root Chakra
In the *Mahanirvana Tantra*, this chakra expresses Earth element with red, and means "base of support" in Sanskrit. It is related to our physical sense of self and being connected to our physical body in a grounded, healthy way. In a **CMLC** viewpoint, it expresses the history of our ancestors, especially how we connect to the generation of our grandparents and great-grandparents in our own individual perspective. It is a place in the body where consciousness without self-awareness resides, in which we follow collective consciousness blueprints of our families and our species.

Located on the area of the perineum, Muladhara is a center of strength in the body. It is also called base chakra or root chakra, and ensures physical health and survival. In the physical body, it rules the excretion systems, the bones, the legs, and the feet.

In the endocrine system, Muladhara governs the adrenals, responsible for our fear and survival hormones and the fight-or-flight response.

In the spinal complex, it rules the tailbone (coccyx).

The sense organ governed by Muladhara is the sense of smell. In aromatherapy, it is balanced with cedar, sandalwood, and cinnamon (LePage and LePage, 2005).

On the emotional level, Muladhara relates to survival issues. When imbalanced, the individual experiences fear of survival and/or fear of death, excessive territoriality, material insecurity, feelings of abandonment, identification with the role of the abandoned child and/or a victim of the circumstances, immobility, disconnection from the physical body, and feelings of being ungrounded and unstable.

On a physical level, possible health challenges related to this chakra are problems with feet, legs, obesity, constipation, phlegm, arthritis, hemorrhoids, and sciatic nerve issues.

On a psychological level, problems with this chakra may include stress, fear of survival, fear of abandonment, phobia, consciousness of scarcity, and lethargy.

When this chakra is working properly, the healthy traits are security, connection to the Earth, vitality, and feeling embodied, responsible, and sufficient, with strong boundaries and the constant experience of being alive and well in the physical body.

On a consciousness level, Muladhara chakra expresses individuality and the "I" as a reference. In **CMLC** perspective, when the energies of ancestors are too present and their lives have been painful, the individual carries these energetic "weights" in the Muladhara chakra.

It is represented in the *Mahanirvana Tantra* writings with four petals that correspond to joy, natural pleasure, bliss that comes from controlling our passions, and happiness that comes from concentration. The key is to keep these four energies balanced without identifying specifically with any of them. When energy is concentrated excessively in any of these "petals," it pulls us away from our center and sense of self, bringing identification with external objects.

Muladhara's four petals symbolize four ways to earthly happiness in Johari's readings of *Mahanirvana Tantra*. Observing our identification with these four forms of happiness can be inspiring for specific types of meditation holding **CMLC** crystals.

Balancing this chakra opens the paths for other chakras to be balanced and moving in a healthy flow. A strong and balanced Muladhara nurtures the other chakras with the energy of the Earth while simultaneously distributing this concentrated energy to balance happiness, health, and well-being in the body.

The four petals symbolize specific energies: Yogananda: happiness in concentration and the bliss of union; Paramananda: maximum joy or the highest bliss of connected consciousness; Virananda: the happiness to control passions, also called "heroic bliss" because it resists temptations; and Sahajananda: natural well-being, also called "innate bliss."

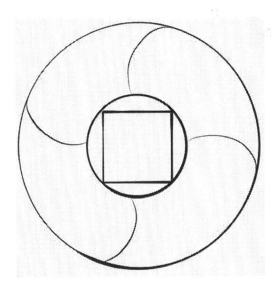

Since the focus of this chakra is on the individual's relationship with self, good energy tools are the practice of Hatha Yoga, walking barefoot, connecting to the Earth, and applying clay or mud on the skin (LePage and LePage 2005).

A good **CMLC** affirmation to balance, strengthen, and expand consciousness and awareness of Muladhara is "I am strong." This keeps us centered and aware, preventing identification with ancestral painful memories and with their difficult life scripts.

The **CMLC** perspective integrates the systemic view of family constellations to the chakras. In the **CMLC** perspective, Muladhara is a portal to connect us to the strength of our paternal and maternal grandparents. The generations that precede our grandparents in the two systems, maternal and paternal, may sometimes vibrate in Swadhisthana and Manipura, but are usually located in the Earth chakra below our feet.

In a healthy, aligned flow of energy, ancestors are seen in this chakra as structural figures in their hierarchical, biological, and social positions as providers of life.

The **CMLC** master crystals to balance, clear, and align Muladhara are red garnet (cubic system), red jasper (trigonal system), and ruby (trigonal system).

Swadhisthana—Sacral or Sexual Chakra
This chakra expresses the energy of water, and the main color in the rainbow spectrum is orange. It means "inner dwelling place" in Sanskrit. It is a center of creativity in the body.

Swadhisthana is related to our unconscious mind, and specifically in a **CMLC** perspective, it expresses the feminine energy of our mother and our individual relationship with her, in our own perspective and subjective inner world. In the **CMLC** is also the original place of our inner child, which is dislocated to the heart when observed, balanced, aligned, and integrated by our life-connection practices. Like Muladhara, Swadhisthana is also a place of collective consciousness.

Swadhisthana chakra expresses the relationship of intimacy between the self and others, and rules all kinds of interpersonal relationships. Located about four finger widths below the navel, it is also called the sacral chakra or the sexual chakra and rules the sex drive, playback and enjoyment of life, and all denser forms of receptivity and assimilation (sexual pleasure, food tasting, and enjoyment of the general physical world).

According to *Mahanirvana Tantra* writings, unlike Muladhara, which expresses sexuality toward the preservation of the species and can be considered the center of sexual energy in men, Swadhisthana is connected to sensuality, the relationship, and pleasure, being the center of sexual energy in women.

In the physical body, it rules the pelvis, the lumbar area, the reproductive system, the urinary system, blood, and lymph.

In the endocrine system, Swadhisthana corresponds to testicles and ovaries, which govern reproduction, and in the spinal complex, it rules the sacrum and the lumbar spine.

The sense organ governed by this chakra is the sense of taste, and it also governs the appetite. In aromatherapy, according to Joseph and Lilian LePage, it is balanced with sage, jasmine, sandalwood, and rose.

On an emotional level, Swadhisthana relates to the continuity of life. When it is imbalanced, the individual experiences sexual imbalance, hypersensitivity or low levels of sensitivity, emotional blockages, unconscious impulses, addictions, compulsions, and imbalance with the rhythms of nature. The person is never satisfied and has the self-image of a martyr.

When this chakra is working properly, the healthy aspects that manifest are balanced sexuality, the ability to feel pleasure on all levels, the ability to feel emotions, continuous integration with the unconscious mind (might be related to what Jung calls the individuation process), healing and overcoming addictions, and harmony with the rhythms of nature. The person connects to his or her own essence of self.

On a physical level, possible health challenges related to Swadhisthana are sexual issues, impotency, frigidity, muscle pain, lumbar pain, insufficient synovial fluid in the joints, PMS, cramps, hot flashes, menopausal symptoms, and womb, bladder, and kidney problems.

On a psychological level, problems with this chakra may include relationship and intimacy issues, shyness, obsessions, compulsions, violence, and eating disorders.

On a consciousness level, Swadhisthana expresses one-to-one relationships—"You and I" as reference. It is represented in the *Mahanirvana Tantra* writings with six petals that correspond to distorted energies that are intrinsic to human nature when we are not aligned and balanced. Identifying with any of these "petals" pulls us away from our center and sense of self, bringing on identification with these distorted energies.

When Swadhisthana is harmonized, it brings satisfaction, joy, creativity, and enthusiasm. There is a natural ability to feel pleasure and genuine emotions, heal addictions, and connect us to the rhythms of nature. We experience the essential self and the peace of being who we are.

According to Johari's understanding of *Mahanirvana Tantra*, this chakra has six petals that can be transcended by the expansion of consciousness and meditation on specific sounds: *Avishvasa* (suspicion); *Prashraya* (indulgence or condescension); *Krurata* (mercilessness); *Sarvanasha* (destructiveness or false knowledge); *Murchchla* (delusion); and *Avajna* (disdain).

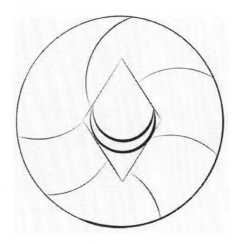

When Swadhisthana becomes balanced, the attributes of its petals are neutralized, and this transparency is called the "truth of the water." When the transparent water is present, the person enjoys tranquility, peace, calm, patience, confidence, and pleasure with everyday details of life and balanced physical senses that can absorb the world more accurately.

Swadhisthana's six petals symbolize six distorted paths of living according to *Mahanirvana Tantra*. Observing our identification with these six forms of distortion can be inspiring forces for meditation to neutralize them.

A healthy focus to heal this chakra is on the individual's relationship with others on a one-on-one level. Good energy healing tools are the practice of Taoism, Qi Gong, Tai Qi Chuan, Tantra Yoga.

A good affirmation for healing, consciousness, and awareness of Swadhisthana is, according to Joseph and Lilian LePage (2005), "I flow freely with the rhythms of life."

By integrating a systems view of family constellations with the chakras, the **CMLC** observes the energy of the person's mother in Swadisthana (not the mother's family system, but the real mother of the individual, her most important traits, and the person's reactions to the mother's personality).

The **CMLC** master crystals to balance, clear, and align Swadisthana are aragonite (orthorhombic system), carnelian (trigonal system), and orange calcite (trigonal system).

Manipura—Solar Plexus Chakra
This chakra expresses the energy of fire with yellow, and it means "city of jewels" in Sanskrit. It is a center of personal power and self-esteem, and specifically in the **CMLC**, it expresses the masculine energy of our father in our own individual perspective. It is also an expression of our ego and the first awakening idea of self-awareness or consciousness of self. The most important aspects of this chakra are the power, fear, anxiety, introversion, rigid belief systems, personal power, and the ability to expand and grow.

Manipura expresses individuality in relationship to others, and it clears the way to allow the personal power of each person to shine. When this chakra is balanced, this self-expression does not overwhelm or overshadow anyone. In the Shakta tradition, personal power means respecting the uniqueness of each person, including self, and understanding that all individuals are equally beautiful and powerful in their potentials.

Manipura expresses the relationship between self and the general social world. It rules self-affirmation as independence and autonomy, expression of one's talents as source of prosperity, and balance in giving and receiving on social levels.

The brightness of Manipura depends on discipline and free will of the individual. The commitment to transcend the destructive nature of its petals is very important when working with Manipura. In this sense, most people do not feel strong enough to engage in such a task and fail to fully live by their own power, which may remain only as nonmanifested potentials.

This chakra governs self-esteem and symbolizes the personal power of each person as it manifests in prosperity. Also called "inner sun," it rules the sense of sight and all organs of metabolic and digestive systems, including the pancreas, the bladder, and the spleen.

Located above the navel and below the breastbone, in the stomach region, this chakra is mentioned in various native cultures of North America as the first physical chakra and is considered the most important chakra for healing physical issues.

In the endocrine system, Manipura corresponds to the pancreas and rules digestion of life in general. In the spinal complex, it is related to the lower thoracic vertebrae, from T8 to T12.

This chakra governs the sense of vision. In aromatherapy, it is balanced with rosemary, geranium, citric oils, and juniper (LePage and LePage, 2005).

On an emotional level, when imbalanced with excessive fire, Manipura corresponds to egotism, selfishness, search for status and fame, Type A personality, imbalanced personal power, discrimination, chronic stress, and unethical behavior. When it is imbalanced with low levels of fire element, it expresses low self-esteem, imbalanced personal power, and isolation tendencies.

When this chakra is working properly, the healthy aspects that manifest are good levels of self-esteem, grounded moral values, balanced personal power, cooperation, acceptance of self and others, balanced use of energy, minimal stress, and ethical behavior.

On a physical level, possible health challenges related to Manipura are lack of energy, digestive issues, liver problems, ulcers, diabetes, hypoglycemia, hypertension, obesity, swollen areas, and inflammation.

On a psychological level, problems with this chakra may include anxiety, rage, narcissism, low self-esteem, feeling disempowered, depression, and shame.

On a consciousness level, Manipura expresses "the spiritual warrior," and when it is out of balance, the person feels like either a slave or a despotic tyrant. When imbalanced, Manipura attracts tyrannical relationships (bullying others or being bullied, alternating slave roles and despot), and the individual acts as a sponge, absorbing all excessive emotional energy of others.

When it is energized and in balance, this chakra acts as a mirror, and our understanding of our social relationships function as smooth surfaces that reflects aspects of our own selves, without judgment, and we can stand in our own identities.

When Manipura is balanced, it brings satisfaction with our individual selves, and we express it in harmony and cooperation—there is no competition. We have a sense that there is room for all people and all talents in the world. When balanced, this chakra brings self-esteem, confidence and prosperity, social integration, cooperation, respect for social values, minimal stress, and ethical behavior.

The person feels inclined to start developing spirituality, restrained attitudes, marital trust, a practical sense of reality, faithfulness, self-esteem, wisdom, and courage. Consequently, the life of the individual will be harmonious. The person feels energized by owning her own life and living according to her own principles, without colliding with social values, experiencing a sense of being in harmony with the world.

This chakra is represented in the *Mahanirvana Tantra* writings with ten petals that correspond to distorted energies that are intrinsic to the nature of Manipura. These petals tend to pull us out of our center when we are not aligned and balanced.

According to Johari's readings of the *Mahanirvana Tantra*, this chakra has ten petals that are balanced by the expansion of consciousness and meditation on specific sounds. These petals are mostly related to spiritual ignorance and are known as *Lajja* (shame); *Pishunata* or *Murkhata* (inconstancy and foolishness); *Irsha* or *Dvesha* (jealousy); *Krurata* (betrayal); *Trishna* (thirst, greed, or desire); *Vishada*, *Udasinata*, or *Duhkha* (sadness); *Kashaya* (boredom); *Moha* or *Bhrama* (spiritual ignorance manifested as illusion); *Ghrina* or *Nirasha* (aversion or disgust); *Bhaya* (fear); *Avidya* (spiritual ignorance).

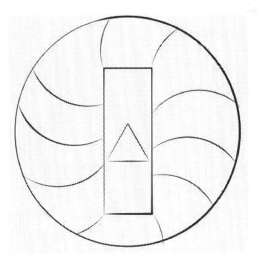

A healthy focus to heal this chakra is on the individual's relationship with his own talents and affirming the value of his work in the world. Good energy-healing tools to balance Manipura are psychotherapy, exercises to develop personal power, Yoga Nidra to reduce stress, and the practice of Karma Yoga. A good affirmation for healing, consciousness, and awareness of Manipura is "I am enough."

In the **CMLC** perspective, Manipura anchors the energy of the father in our bodies and how that relationship is processed in the person's energy field.

The three main crystals to balance Manipura in a **CMLC** perspective are golden rutile (tetragonal system), golden tigereye (trigonal system), and citrine (trigonal system).

Anahata—Heart Chakra
This chakra is associated with air element and means "untouched" in Sanskrit. It is a center of love in the body—love of self, love of others, and love for humanity.

It is originally represented in *Mahanirvana Tantra* writings in earthy cinnabar and white and dry green colors. Contemporary spirituality often uses pink and bright emerald green to represent it. Sometimes represented only with the emerald-green color. Air element is expressed in Anahata, where our higher conscious individuality and personal truth awaken.

In Anahata we feel the integration of our unique selves with the world and others, especially with humanity. Through this chakra we also connect to forces of nature, minerals, plants, and animals.

Located in the sternum, right between the breasts, Anahata rules blood circulation and the lower respiratory system.

In the endocrine system, Anahata connects to the thymus chakra (described in more detail below) and rules unconditional love, love for self, and love for others.

The sense organ governed by this chakra is the sense of touch. In aromatherapy, it is balanced with rose, jasmine, lavender, and orange (LePage and Lepage, 2005). In the spinal complex, it is related to the upper thoracic vertebrae, from T1 to T7.

On an emotional level, when it is imbalanced in an active state of intensity, Anahata corresponds with conditional love, being closed to the world, and being armored, judgmental, critical, cynical, cruel, individualistic, unforgiving, and distrustful. When this chakra is imbalanced with low levels of energy in a passive state, it expresses depression, sadness, self-neglect, and feeling troubled, isolated from the natural world, and in fear of rejection.

When working properly, Anahata expresses healthy aspects such as open-heartedness, unconditional love, and feeling cheerful, compassionate, friendly, self-caring, peaceful at heart, altruistic, hopeful, ecological, humanistic, receptive, forgiving, and confident.

On a physical level, possible health challenges related to Anahata are asthma, alcoholism, lung disease, circulation issues, atherosclerosis, high blood pressure, chest pain, and heart disease.

On a psychological level, problems with this chakra may include codependency, depression, anxiety, isolation, solitude, fear of connection to others, and fear of commitment.

On a consciousness level, Anahata expresses what many contemporary schools of spirituality call "Higher Self." It relates to a loving attitude, and the person feels like a living part of humanity if this chakra is balanced. When it is imbalanced, there is a feeling of being an impostor and/or feeling constantly abused.

Anahata is represented in the *Mahanirvana Tantra* writings with twelve petals that are "contaminated" by distorted energies that are intrinsic to human nature and specific of the possible distortions of Anahata. They need to be neutralized for life to flow in a healthy way. These petals tend to pull us out of our center when we are not aligned and balanced.

According to Johari's readings of *Mahanirvana Tantra*, this chakra can be balanced by the expansion of consciousness and meditation on specific sounds that help with the mental modifications that neutralize specific petals: *Asha* (hope); *Chinta* (excessive care and anxiety); *Cheshta* (intense effort); *Mamata* (possessiveness); *Dambha* (arrogance); *Vikalata* (fragility, inertia, or incompetence); *Ahangkara* (discrimination); *Viveka* (cupidity, selfishness or avarice); *Lolata* (lust); *Kapatata* (rebellion and fraud); *Vitarka* (indecision); *Anutapa* (regret).

The most important aspects of the psyche related to this chakra are passionate enthusiasm, tenderness, the inner child, unconditional love, compassion, devotion, and acceptance. When imbalanced, this chakra expresses rejection.

Anahata balance brings a feeling that everything that makes us unique is respected and in harmony with the universe, and that is when we can join with and welcome others. In Anahata, we feel the truth and our personal feelings, and we also accept the feelings of others. This is where true compassion begins.

Located at the heart level, this chakra is linked to the sense of touch and the thymus gland, although there is a specific thymus chakra as well. The Anahata governs the immune, circulatory, and lymphatic systems, including the heart and lungs, as well as the shoulders, arms and hands, thoracic spine, and shoulder blades.

According to Shakta wisdom, Anahata chakra has twelve petals, and if we can transcend them, we can neutralize the characteristics printed on the petals of this chakra so the person can breathe and be transparent. The petals represent lust, desire, trickery, indecision, repentance, hope, anxiety, impartiality, arrogance, incompetence, discrimination, and defiance (rebellion). Are all reactions to times when we are wounded emotionally, crystallizing the pain on its petals.

When imbalanced, Anahata brings feelings and behaviors of armoring, conditional love, criticism, depression, sadness, self-neglect, heavy heart, cynicism, and cruelty, separation from nature, individualism, fear of rejection, inability to forgive, mistrust, bitterness, rancor, codependency, alcoholism, anxiety, and fear. One feels permanently like an impostor. The body presents symptoms such as asthma, bronchitis, emphysema, lung cancer, heart disease, arteriosclerosis, high blood pressure, tachycardia, and chest pain.

When balanced, from Anahata flows a feeling of love, trust, and emotional healing. The person experiences an open heart, unconditional love, compassion, good humor, self-care, peace, tranquility, altruism, trust in the processes of life, faith, humanism, harmony with nature, responsiveness, ease in forgiveness, and the ability to forget emotional pain. There is a feeling of being an important part of humanity.

The **CMLC** considers also that in Anahata the physical and spiritual dimensions come together in the human individual and manifest synthesis of our unique being in the present moment. This is a chakra hybrid or mixed nature, both physical and spiritual, both human and divine. A good affirmation to balance and strengthen this chakra in a **CMLC** practice is "I am love."

The three basic crystals that balance Anahata are green tourmaline (trigonal system), rose quartz (trigonal system), and diopside (monoclinic system).

Ananda, or Thymus Chakra
Ananda means "the space of happiness" in Sanskrit. It is an additional lotus or smaller chakra located within Anahata, on the right side of the physical heart. This additional chakra represents the "spiritual" or "etheric" heart.

Ananda emanates inspirations of sublime art and contemplation of beauty. It feels like a haven of peace where the inner guidance within each of us rests. Ananda is a fundamental space for the **CMLC**, corresponding to the direction "within" and "the now" in Native American cultures. It also included the cardinal directions that are similar to the medicine wheel in Native American cultures. In the **CMLC**, all healing comes from honesty and the truth of the soul and the heart, which is in Ananda.

In the **CMLC**, this space preserves our joy or brings us back to it. It is a well of endless happiness and fulfillment, and therefore, a storehouse of health and healing. Ananda connects us to the present moment and corresponds to the thymus chakra and the immune system. It brings a message that the happier we are (and happiness comes mostly from living from the truth), the healthier we are.

According to Johari, it is untouched by physical impurities. Ananda is the location of self-awareness of the awakened consciousness and of the awareness in our dream states. It is supposedly the "temple of God" (Johari, 2000).

This chakra vibrates in light-green, teal, and aqua colors and is sometimes called "the higher heart." The thymus gland is a portal of the energy of happiness, which comes forth primarily when we share our truth and love with mankind.

A good affirmation to strengthen this chakra is "I am happiness."

In the **CMLC**, Ananda is balanced with green fluorite (cubic system) and green kunzite (monoclinic system).

Vishuddha—Throat Chakra

This chakra is associated with ether element, or space. Vishuddha is a spiritual chakra that in Sanskrit means "purification." Located at the throat level, it is associated with the celestial-blue and bright-blue tones.

This chakra is connected to the thyroid gland and the sense of hearing, revealing the relationship between self and the spirit. Vishuddha allows self-expression and communication and governs the neck, ears, nostrils, teeth, mouth, and tongue.

It is a center of personal truth in the body. Originally represented in *Mahanirvana Tantra* writings in turquoise and white colors, it is where individuality and personal truth manifest. In Anahata we awaken to our individuality silently, and in Vishuddha, we express our personal truth and self-awareness.

Vishuddha rules the upper respiratory system and the sense of hearing. In the spinal complex, it is related to the lower cervical vertebrae, from C3 to C7.

In the endocrine system, it governs the thyroid, and in aromatherapy it is balanced with lemongrass, frankincense, eucalyptus, and pine. (LePage and LePage, 2005).

On an emotional level, when it is imbalanced in an active state of intensity, we tend to lie, talk too much, speak half-truths, and use violent words.

When this chakra is imbalanced with low levels of energy in a passive state, it expresses lack of faith, lack of purpose, blocked intuition and lack of discipline.

When working properly, Vishuddha expresses healthy possibilities of creativity and rejuvenation.

THE CARDINAL METHOD OF LIFE CONNECTION

Vishuddha is represented in the *Mahanirvana Tantra* writings with sixteen petals that are pure by nature and bring no distorted energies intrinsic to the human condition. Specific distortions related to this chakra come from "contamination" from the outside world.

According to Johari's understanding of the *Mahanirvana Tantra*, this chakra can be balanced by the expansion of consciousness and meditation on specific sounds that help with mental modifications that neutralize the petals, which may eventually be contaminated by external forces.

Since Vishuddha does not have any intrinsically negative elements but is vulnerable to external negative energies and influences, in a **CMLC** perspective, it is especially vulnerable to cruelty. Its nature exudes the pure light of spirit, but if the cruelties of the outside world contaminate this chakra, or if distorted energies from Swadhisthana, Manipura, and Anahata flow up the Sushumna channel and reach Vishuddha, we become inhibited, isolated, and unable to express ourselves authentically.

The previous three chakras (Anahata, Manipura and Swadhisthana) are not externally influenced by design—they contain in themselves the ability to neutralize the distortions of the mind (*vrittis*) and express clear energy in their own natures. We can transmute the energies of these three chakras daily with meditation, prayer, and energetic cleansing practices, such as the use of crystals. The higher spiritual chakras, Vishudda, Ajna, and Sahashara, on the other hand, naturally emanate only the light of spirit, but they can become distorted by the energies of the environment, and by traumatic individual experiences that lead us to engage in a dualistic perspective of separation.

The best thing a person can do to purify his or her life is to transcend the innate disharmonizing energies of Swadhisthana, Manipura, and Anahata with a conscious effort of free will, or to surrender to a spiritual path. When it is possible to neutralize these interferences, the petals of the higher chakras become clear and transparent. The more we purify them, the easier it is to connect to higher levels of consciousness, light, and the natural flow of life.

The sixteen Vishuddha petals express sacred sounds. One of them is the mantra *Om*, seven of them express the mantras assigned to other chakras, and seven express the seven main musical tones. The sixteenth petal corresponds to the sweetness (Johari, 2000). The nature of Vishuddha is to express higher vibrations through sounds and the conquest of the challenges of Muladhara, whose four petals correspond to harmonious energies.

When contaminated, Vishuddha expresses violence with brutal, cruel, and unclean words, lies, the false need to appear more than we really are, waste of energy by talking too much, addictions, intoxication, lack of hope, lack of discipline, spiritual blindness, disability, lack of faith and purpose, lack of intuition, a freezing feeling, difficulty to maintain spiritual practices and to dedicate ourselves to our true calling, communication difficulties, biased perspectives, skeptical behavior, and disbelief. The body manifests symptoms such as sore throats, tonsillitis, laryngitis, thyroid problems, hearing issues, and metabolism imbalances.

When harmonized and purified, Vishuddha expresses nonviolence, truth, a consciousness of not stealing, the ability to conserve energy, detachment, purification, contentment, discipline, self-connection and self-awareness, the ability to overcome obstacles, appropriate judgments, the ability to experience neutrality, playfulness, delivery, awareness of our mission, and faith. We feel comfortable in the role of a spiritual seeker and address life from a space of calm proactivity.

In the **CMLC** perspective, in Vishuddha we find the strength of the blossoming to life, which is a process that can be compared to blooming flowers. Beauty and true power, which is the power of meaningful words, are expressed by our true voice in all its manifestations (talk, speech, music, work). A good **CMLC** affirmation to balance this chakra is "I am truth."

The three basic crystals that balance Vishuddha are amazonite (triclinic system), aquamarine (hexagonal system), and blue qartz (trigonal system).

Ajna—Frontal Chakra, or Third Eye

Ajna is the sixth chakra and expresses itself with the colors violet or indigo blue. Located in the center of the forehead, Ajna represents light and means "point of command" in Sanskrit. It is connected to the pituitary gland, the eyes, and the hypothalamus (considered the emotional center of the brain), the regulation of the endocrine and nervous systems, and what we call the "sixth sense."

In aromatherapy, Ajna is balanced with lavender and violet essences (LePage and LePage, 2005). In the spinal complex, it is related to C2.

When imbalanced, it may cause physical symptoms such as foggy eyes, neurological problems, headaches, and nightmares.

Since Ajna means "control point" in Sanskrit, it has the power to balance masculine and feminine in perfect synthesis. This chakra has only two petals connected to a central circle, symbolizing the integration of the two hemispheres of the brain and a space for Higher Consciousness. In Ajna, Higher Consciousness awakens.

We feel and know the truth of the world with absolute clarity when this chakra is balanced and strong. In Ajna lies the sense of reality beyond physical matter and the insight that comes from the fact that what is inside our internal world creates what is outside of us. Illusions and distortions can be easily discerned and clearly seen when Ajna is balanced.

When imbalanced, Ajna causes feelings of dependency and pride regrading theoretical or intellectual knowledge. It also manifests attachment and identification with spiritual experiences and feelings of intellectual and spiritual superiority, which is a common trap to gurus or people who are isolated from the world, disqualifying all those who do not agree with their ideas.

The physical body may manifest eye problems, headaches, nightmares, eyestrain, obscured vision, and neurological problems. One becomes skeptical and disqualifying, leading to a lack of awareness of the real and true spiritual dimension of life, replaced by intellectualized concepts or even the practice of negative magic.

When balanced, Ajna strengthens our ability to maintain awareness in self-connection processes, and to remain steady as an observer or witness of our own processes in the center of our being, in and the center of every experience, without identification with titles or roles.

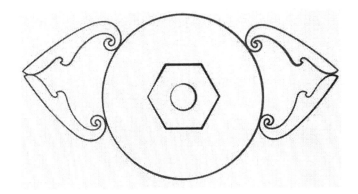

We remain invulnerable to paralysis in the events that occur. Ajna brings balance between the lower, primitive aspects of the self and the more evolved, pure aspects of the Higher Self. We develop confidence in our intuition and may feel like a yogi in peace and tranquility by the expansion of awareness and inclusion of the whole universe in our lives, experiencing intuition, clarity, and meditation. A good **CMLC** affirmation to strengthen this chakra is "I am aware."

In the **CMLC** the basic crystals to balance Ajna are sugilite (hexagonal system), lapis lazuli (isometric system), and amethyst (trigonal system).

Sahashara—Crown Chakra
The Sanskrit meaning of Sahashara is "a thousand petals." Its colors are platinum, white, or clear crystal, and it is symbolized as a lotus of a thousand petals of crystalline light with a sphere in the center. Sahashara is located at the top of the head. Like Muladhara, which directs its energy to and from the Earth in a vertical direction, it directs energy to and from the sky within the physical body. The other chakras are connected in the horizontal direction and have outlets in the front and back of the body.

This chakra is the expression of God connection, unity, and silence. It does not have a mantra sound and is beyond the elements and the senses. In the physical body, it is linked to the pineal gland, and it regulates all cellular and genetic levels.

In the spinal complex, Sahashara is connected to C1, and in aromatherapy, it is balanced with the essence of lotus.

When imbalanced, Sahashara causes mental disorders by the feeling of separation from the divine. Emotional instability related to Sahashara can be expressed by identification with disease and a mistaken attitude of disease as the real source of the "I am" consciousness.

When balanced, this chakra promotes the release of karma, strengthens universal consciousness, and promotes a feeling of fulfillment. We easily connect to transcendental consciousness and deep states of meditation. There is a feeling of integration with the physical body that goes beyond images or appearance on the material level. Dense physical matter and our subtle, Higher Self aspect are merged as part of the same substance.

While Ajna promotes understanding of diversity, the myriad levels of creation and existence, discernment between reality and illusion, and separating wheat from chaff, Sahashara goes beyond dichotomies and plurality. When we connect to this chakra in its full potential, we feel all creation as synthesis and absolutely integrated in unity. Through this chakra we fall into a state of enlightenment and wisdom.

A good affirmation to strengthen this chakra is "I am connected." The practice of meditation, prayer, and devotion strengthen Sahashara. It is the place where God Most High communicates with our divine aspect within, which resides in the heart.

In the **CMLC**, the basic crystals that connect Sahashara are clear quartz (trigonal system), apophyllite (tetragonal system), and diamond (isometric system).

6

INDIVIDUAL ASPECTS OF THE PSYCHE

Each person is unique in his or her own internal world. We manifest our creativity and our distortions and "spiritual errors" in very specific ways, which is why we can use different systems of knowledge to explore ourselves within.

When we commit to connection with self and with a life-connection path, it is important to be aware of the aspects of our psyches. Since our inner world is vast and very complex, there are many internal areas and aspects of our psyches to be explored.

When we observe the psyche from a **CMLC** perspective, some aspects are important to understand and integrate. We especially need to observe which aspects of the psyche are explicitly or secretly ruling our lives.

Internal Alignment of the Inner Child, the Ego, the Soul, the Real Self, and the Higher Self
Some aspects of the psyche are substantial, such as the emotions, inner child, and the soul; others are processors of information that are guided by the substantial and/or the essential aspects, such as the ego and the rational, cognitive mind; and others are essential, such our spirits and real selves.

We will now look at some of the most important aspects of the individual psyche for the **CMLC**.

Inner Child
The inner child is the aspect of ourselves that preserves the elements of our childhood and who we were as children. A healthy inner child preserves the natural qualities of a child within us, which are innocence, joy, purity, and grace. A wounded inner child, however, stores memories of emotional pain and can be a very destructive unconscious force in the psyche.

Our inner child is easily wounded and reacts immediately. Depending on the person, the inner child may hold on to emotional wounds and allow these wounds to rule the person's life throughout adulthood.

Our inner child is very systemic, meaning it is deeply connected to the collective unconscious mind of the family soul. Depending on the person, the inner child feels and expresses collective wounds of ancestors and tends to react to painful experiences with promises of vengeance.

The inner child does not have the power to observe, only to react. When we take the time to hold a crystal, close our eyes, and focus on our inner child as we breathe deeply, a lot of information may surface, and this may be the key to releasing many blockages in our lives.

Individual Soul
The family soul is collective, and the individual soul merges with the soul of the family. The moment a child is conceived, the soul of that child will connect with the soul of the family and carry all its contents.

Like the inner child, the individual soul can also be very sensitive to the contents of the energetic environment around it. It will absorb all kinds of contents depending on how aware and vulnerable the individual soul is.

If we take the time to hold a crystal and focus on our individual soul as we breathe deeply, we may heal many "wounded patches" just by doing this practice. With the soul information may not arise like it does with the inner child, but the soul heals very fast with the silent presence of crystals.

The Place of the Child in Family Systems and the Work of Tarso Firace

Tarso Firace is a Brazilian physicist who, inspired by the work of David Bohm, observes how consciousness operates and how self-awareness awakens within family systems (Firace, 2014). He combines quantum physics, family constellations, the chakra system, and the light within to suggest a unique type of awareness that can help us understand not only ourselves, but also members of our family and people in our intimate social circles.

Firace has been researching the connections between quantum physics, collective family consciousness, and the chakras system for over thirty years. He has developed a vision in which matter, energy, and light express themselves in family fields, and which describes how this relates to the structure of the chakras system.

Using Einstein's formula $E=mc^2$—energy equals mass times the speed of light squared—the speed of light squared is, in Firace's perspective, consciousness. In Firace's work, consciousness travels through matter and energy and becomes light in its exponential state. When it comes to the family system, the first child born is called Alpha and will express the consciousness of matter and manifestation. The second child is called Beta and will manifest the consciousness of energy and feeling. The third child is called Gama and will manifest the consciousness of light and understanding. Firace organizes his system by observing how, in his perspective, energy rises in a family system from the lower chakras and repeats itself in the Alpha-Beta-Gama pattern.

When matter, energy, and light are superimposed upon the chakra system, matter governs the root chakra and relates to action. Energy governs the sacral chakra and relates to feeling. Light governs the solar plexus and relates to understanding. The first three chakras are physical and correspond to the position of each new child that arrives in a family. The position of each child corresponds to each chakra and its specific attributes, as if the family had a "collective body" with corresponding "collective chakras."

In Firace's perspective, children who arrive in the family system are counted by "the seed of the Father." In his model, to count the number of children and their place in the family system, it does not matter how many times the mother has been pregnant, because the children are counted in the father's system. This does not mean that the mother is not important. It means that in the interaction between mother and father, the mother represents the Earth and the continuity of energy, and the father represents the sky and the creation of new energy.

Counting the children and where they are placed follows a counting system in which the father creates children that belong to a specific structure. In this model, the first child of the father is an Alpha, and expresses matter and action, revealing qualities of the root chakra. In this perspective, action is an expression of survival.

The second child is Beta and represents energy. This child expresses feeling and physical connection, revealing the qualities of the sacral chakra. In this perspective, this relates to emotional expressions.

The third child is Gama and represents light. This child expresses mental understanding, revealing qualities of the solar plexus.

In this perspective, this relates to awareness, expanded vision, and discernment.

In Firace's understanding, once light manifests in a family system, after a third child is conceived, the family starts seeing with the heart. Vision goes beyond seeing physical matter, images, and appearances, and the heart energy is activated. The heart sees vibrations, and a broader, new level of understanding is created in the family soul. The second Alpha child will manifest the qualities of the heart chakra and manifest a leadership based on heart connections.

When a fourth child is born, the Alpha-Beta-Gama pattern repeats itself. This fourth child is another Alpha, but in a higher vibration of the heart chakra, which includes light, emotions, and action.

The fifth child will be a second Beta, expressing the qualities of Vishuddha in the family system, accumulating the energy of the previous chakras. The sixth child is a second Gama and expresses the qualities of Ajna, accumulating the energy that has already been manifested in the previous chakras. The seventh child is a third Alpha, bringing the energy of the system back to the root chakra, because Sahashara is the place of Omega consciousness, where we transcend the human condition. The eighth child is a Beta child and so forth.

The quality of the energy and where it is placed is important for internal alignment and collective soul alignment. For example, a person may have an unborn brother, who is the Alpha child in the system, even if this child was not born. The next child is a biological Beta, but since he or she is the first child that is born, he or she becomes a social Alpha, even if that is not the truth of the family soul. This person will express intrinsic characteristics of Beta, but will occupy the place of an Alpha child, which is emotionally challenging.

This "social misplacement" of biological order causes confusion in both the individual soul and the family soul, and it is very common to see these types of problems being revealed and solved in family constellations.

In the **CMLC** experience, crystals align the energy and consistently bring peace to the mind and heart, the more they are used with this purpose. Crystals are very efficient when used with an intention to realign the soul with the truth.

The Ego
The ego is a step forward toward evolution in the human condition; it is closer to an individuation process and is more capable of observing. When balanced, the ego is important to give us a sense of individuality, but when predominant, it leads us to isolation and separation, and our energy nurtures the subjective inner world described by Thomas Hobbes.

The ego is in the right place when we assert ourselves in the world and cultivate healthy boundaries. It is not balanced and is overreactive when we become either too controlling and imposing, leading us to isolation.

In a **CMLC** perspective, the root of isolation of the inner child is usually fear, and the root of isolation from the ego is usually suspicion that leads to anger.

The ego gives us a sense of individuality. It is part of the human condition and an aspect of what we can call a "localized consciousness" (Veltheim and Muiznieks, 2013). It becomes distorted when this sense of individuality, freedom, and autonomous energy reaffirms a sense of separation. The ego does not create the sense of separation, but when it charges the ego, it becomes distorted. When the Higher Self inspires the ego, it helps us get things done and becomes an ally in accomplishing our life purposes. The major goal is to merge the ego and the higher self in a synthesis process so we become whole as a person, one with the universe and one with God.

The ego doesn't want to surrender. It makes us play small and gets us thinking that we are playing big, but that is an illusion because it compares us to others to create images of superiority that are not real.

In a **CMLC** perspective, the inner child is an emotional expression of our dualistic human condition, and the ego is its mental expression. The inner child has no real sense of autonomy and tends to be symbiotic. The ego has such an extreme sense of individuality that, if in charge of the psyche, leads to separation and isolation.

Both the inner child and the ego, if in charge of the psyche, can be extremely self-centered, but they also depend on others to fulfill their desires. The inner child demands attention and wants to be taken care of. It needs to belong to specific groups of people it chooses (usually as projections of the family of origin) at any price, even if that social group is hostile and limiting to the free flow of life.

The ego wants to control all situations and has different strategies to control others, and these strategies, such as manipulation or explicit power struggles may come from an unconscious motivation to assert personal power with individualistic and megalomaniac purposes. It promotes separation and isolation.

A healthy ego understands its job and place is not to rule the psyche but to serve the more evolved aspects of our inner world, which are the real self and the Higher Self. When the ego serves itself, life has no purpose except personal power in a destructive way, which leads to a feeling of lack of a higher purpose in the end. When the ego serves the inner child, it tends to be weak, and the adult person lives like a child in one aspect or other, such as emotional or monetary dependency on others.

Real Self
The real self is the person we are essentially when we are living from the truth, and not from trauma or family loyalty. It is the human aspect of our psyche that expresses our uniqueness and individuality as a synthesis of the most original characteristics of our parents and ancestors.

The real self is the human expression of our truth and joy of life. It is an essence that lives in the heart, a creative source of energy that connects to others in benign relationships and creates beauty in the world. Many of us are not in touch with the real self because we are too entangled in the needs of the inner child, the emotional pain of the soul, or the controlling mechanisms of the ego.

In the **CMLC** perspective, crystals are a great tool to help us connect to the real self. They align our consciousness with the truth of our being and allow us to get past the distracting interferences of the mind, inner child, and ego. When we hold a crystal, close our eyes, and focus on the truth of our being with an allowing attitude, the truth of our real selves will surface, and we can recognize that from the flow of lightness and joy that invades our being.

Higher Self
The Higher Self is the presence of God within us. It has the highest vibrations within the psyche and speaks from higher realms with kind authority. When we are connected to the Higher Self, we are not expressing our uniqueness, but collective virtues and higher vibrational energies such as unconditional love, truth, grace, peace, faith, trust, and good will.

The Higher Self is strengthened by dedication to a spiritual life, spiritual reading and devotional practices, prayers, meditation, silence and fasting. It manifests itself through a clear mind and inspired action. The Higher Self speaks to us and to the world in a silent, loving presence, or with very few words that bring depth of soul and consciousness expansion. The less we speak, the more we connect to and are guided by the Higher Self, and the closer we are to God.

The Higher Self manifests the highest vibrations of cosmic consciousness. If our inner world is noisy and ruled by the inner child, the wounded soul, or the ego, we are not connected to the Higher Self and may not develop the senses to feel its presence.

Spiritual and angelic crystals, such as angelite, celestite, amethyst, rose quartz, citrine, and selenite, help us connect to the Higher Self. When we hold them in silence with a pure intention to feel this connection, it may happen gradually or suddenly. We must have the clear intention and the diligent practice to establish and maintain this connection.

The Cardinal Method of Life Connection and the Aspects of the Psyche

The purpose of the **CMLC** is precisely to organize the psyche so that life can flow in all its abundance into and through our being. We use information and crystals as tools to help this clearing and connection.

The **CMLC** is an educational system. Its intention is to inform the soul of its contents and encourage us to awaken our real selves and the spiritual area of our lives. When we learn about the inner child, the soul, the ego, the real self, and the higher self, our minds begin to awaken to aspects that are not only functional and operational. As we expand our minds with knowledge about purpose and meaning, life becomes richer, brighter, healthier, and full of joy and fulfillment.

Our commitment to create a better life path should be both theoretical and practical. As we educate our minds and souls, we also need energetic tools and practices to ensure that we are strengthening our awareness and maintaining an allowing, receptive attitude, and at the same time, preserving our healthy boundaries.

The last chapter of this book will give a quick and profound practice with crystals that includes a sacred geometric structure to connect us to the best of life.

7

ALIGNING OUR INNER WORLDS WITH THE POWER OF CRYSTALS

Before we start the practice, the last thing that is important to understand is that as human beings, we have three major levels of consciousness. The levels of consciousness coexist as we move forward and upward in the expansion-of-consciousness scale. It is important to pay attention to what we read in these last pages and hold a crystal as we read them.

Three Levels of Consciousness
We can observe the three levels of consciousness from a dialectic perspective. Bert Hellinger speaks of three levels of consciousness by naming them "collective, individual, and universal." The first level is the group consciousness of the family and culture. It is automatic and a given of the human condition. In my **CMLC** observations and research, I have come to realize that some people never leave this level of consciousness and remain "expressions" of their family beliefs and patterns, and of their nationality and culture. This is not a judgment or disqualification—it is an observation. People have very different timing to engage in self-discovery and self-connection processes, and this should be respected.

The second level of consciousness, in Hellinger's understanding, is the individual awareness of an autonomous, independent self that takes the strength from the family and culture and expands the horizons of life. This means the person moves forward, expanding awareness of self, creating a rich inner world, and contributing to the world and humanity.

The third level of consciousness in Hellinger's perspective is universal consciousness, in which the independent, fulfilled individual feels part of humanity and transcends a consciousness of individuality. There are no "selective affections," as David Hume would say (Hume, 1875, 1985)), and each human being, living being, and inanimate object on the planet is seen and treated with respect and as part of that person's existence. Universal consciousness encompasses indiscriminate, unconditional, universal love for humanity.

The **CMLC** adopts this idea of three levels of consciousness described in the first chapter of this book. As said before, the concepts used in the **CMLC** are **functional consciousness, individual consciousness**, and **Higher Consciousness**.

The functional state of consciousness permeates all creation, including inanimate objects. There is consciousness at work in every particle of the manifested universe, but it is not aware of itself. The archaic consciousness of the soul described in family constellations operates on that level.

Functional consciousness follows an energetic movement blueprint that creates a flow of existence, but this flow is not self-aware. Objects, biological matter and microscopic beings, plants, and animals are in this category, since consciousness is a prerequisite to existence and physical manifestation, and *consciousness is all there is*. In the **CMLC** perspective, we automatically live this state of consciousness because it is the very essence, the immediate given, or thesis in a dialectic process of human existence.

Individual consciousness can be considered an antithesis of functional consciousness and is potentially present in all human beings. Different people have distinct levels of self-awareness, but all human beings, regardless of their levels of personal development, has some percentage of individual consciousness, even if it is not developed.

Individual awareness of self can manifest in many layers and levels. It is a gradual, dialectic, expanding, spiraling process that requires commitment and endurance, because in a way, developing self-awareness can be compared to going against gravity in a material state of being.

Self-awareness requires time, so that the individual can have a reference of self-development. It is continuous and progressive, but it does take time. The idea of time brings a different sensation compared to the slumbering state of consciousness, in which animate and inanimate beings automatically follow an energetic blueprint of movement and flow.

The third stage of consciousness is a leap into universal awareness and a direct connection with God. **Higher Consciousness** surpasses self-awareness and becomes universal awareness, where there is no separation and no concept of time.

When we reach a stage of purification and living in truth with self and others, we are ready to engage in this state of consciousness. To be in this state, we must absolutely discard the possibility of avoidance, which throws us in a state of separation. We need and want to know the deepest truth of all there is, and thus merge with the universal state of cosmic being.

Consciousness and Crystal Systems in the CMLC
In the **CMLC**, the three levels of consciousness are present in the crystal systems and are also related to our family systems, to the environment we are in, to the chakras, and to the aspects of our psyches.

Starting with the family soul, the **CMLC** observes it as a collective entity with an archaic consciousness that ideally follows a geometric blueprint. When there are disorders and distortions in the family soul, crystals can help align them with the healthy, natural blueprint of its functional consciousness.

Regarding our physical bodies, da Vinci's Vitruvian Man is a strong reference for the **CMLC**. When we observe the interaction of the ideal proportions and geometry of the human body blueprint, we can observe the interaction of the internal geometry of crystals and how it can influence the energetic blueprint of the functional consciousness of the physical body to bring it back to alignment.

In the **CMLC**, the seven crystal systems are associated with the seven main chakras in the body. As said before in chapter 2 of this book, crystals are grouped in thirty-two classes and seven structured systems. The **CMLC** observes coherence between the seven crystal systems and the seven chakras

In a **CMLC** understanding, cubic system crystals align Muladhara. It corresponds to the collective and to the slumbering state of consciousness so that it works properly, like a machine that functions well. The internal geometry of these crystals strengthens physical matter, which includes the healthy survival of our physical bodies, and aligns our relationships with our grandparents.

The orthorhombic system crystals align Swadhisthana, which is also related to the collective and the slumbering state of consciousness. They especially connect us to the pleasure of being alive. The internal geometry of these crystals clears our emotions and allows us to feel with more flow, instead of holding on to grudges or developing emotional attachments. They also purify and align the visceral relationship we all have with our mothers, clearing away symbiotic energy chords we may still hold with them, and allowing us to take their strength.

The tetragonal system crystals align Manipura and awaken the first stages of individual consciousness and self-awareness, which begin with the use of our rational mind. These crystals elevate our minds to individual self-awareness and purify the ego. They also clear our relationship with our father, especially energies of competition, and encourage us to take the strength of the father.

Monoclinic system crystals align Anahata and initiate a more elevated state of self-awareness, which includes love in a higher state. It is where the level of self-awareness consciousness begins, which paves the way for universal or cosmic consciousness to awake. The internal geometry of these crystals encourages love for self, love for others, and unconditional love for humankind, the world, and nature.

The triclinic system crystals align Vishuddha, which is the lower of the three main spiritual chakras in the body. They intensify the state of self-awareness and simultaneously connect us with a symmetric relationship between self-awareness and the functional state of consciousness, which should be structured and aligned for Vishuddha to work well and express the truth in all its vitality. It is a prelude to the cosmic state of consciousness.

Hexagonal system crystals align Ajna. The hexagonal format brings perfect balance to the left and right hemispheres of the brain, as well and balance between Earth and sky on a cosmic level. The internal geometry of these crystals brings clarity of mind and an ability to make connections. They engage us in cosmic awareness or universal consciousness regarding the world and the universe.

The trigonal system crystals align Sahashara and connect us with pure universal consciousness, bringing full awareness of God within and of God, creator of all that is. The trigonal system is very special because its internal geometry is always threefold, creating pyramids, but these are unpredictable and creative. This crystal system connects us to universal consciousness on a higher level and with dimensions beyond what the conscious mind can fathom.

The **CMLC** associates three main crystals with each chakra to balance them. To align all chakras with cosmic consciousness in the **CMLC**, there is always a crystal from the trigonal system, as a reminder of cosmic consciousness and the highest chakra level of Sahashara, so that all chakras are always connected to the crown chakra through the Sushumna channel to reinforce the God connection in every level of our being.

Consciousness Levels, Chakras, and Crystals in the CMLC
The **CMLC** associates crystal systems with the chakras in a perspective that includes family systems.

In the **CMLC**, Muladhara corresponds to the energy of our grandparents present in our bodies, Swadhisthana to our mother, and Manipura to our father. The first two lower chakras relate to functional consciousness. When energy arrives at Manipura, the functional state remains and coexists with the introduction of self-awareness with the presence of the father.

In Manipura we begin to connect to our consciousness of self-awareness and affirm the understanding of who we are as individuals. Manipura is a processor of our consciousness of individuality, which is both functional and existential. It is where we begin to build our self-esteem.

If the lower physical chakras are not harmonized, it is unlikely that we will be able to discern our own feelings from the feelings of other members of the family of origin, and from the feelings of our ancestors present in our bodies.

The **CMLC** considers that Swadhisthana expresses our relationship with our mother, and Manipura, with our father. In Anahata we store our individual experiences and the sufferings of our personal life journey. If we connect to self-awareness consciousness in this chakra, purity and the genuine feelings of the child's innocence can be preserved for life if Anahata is always balanced and clear.

In Anahata, consciousness of self-awareness predominates. We align with this consciousness of self-awareness and feel love for who we are, love for others, and love for the universe.

Anahata is extremely important to the **CMLC** because it is the acceptance of all there is in our personal and collective journey. We surrender to God, to our family problems, to all limitations, to the unconscious arrogance of the inner child, to the root of our attachments, and to our resistance to the destiny of each member of our family. In Anahata we have the first opportunities to surrender, consent, and transcended all that is, so we can be free to follow our own paths. It is one of the keys for change and expansion.

In Vishuddha consciousness of self-awareness in love unfolds into a deeper understanding of the truth. This is ideally where we fully connect to self-awareness in love and truth, where we express our individuality and unique creative abilities, and where we begin to connect to cosmic consciousness.

Ajna is where we begin to reach cosmic consciousness—where it coexists with self-awareness and functional consciousness. It is the first level of awakening to a state that incorporates and transcends our individuality. Ajna is a key place of discernment of energy, where we get clarity of what belongs to us and what belongs to others, and how the internal world is creating what we experience in the external world.

Sahashara is a place of complete surrender, where cosmic consciousness resides in the body. It is a place of silence in which the potential of absolute integration with all there is may manifest within us. Sahashara integrates all levels of consciousness and transcends time. It is the place of Omega, in Firace's words (Firace, 2014). The state of Omega is beyond time, space, and separation. It is a state of unity and bliss.

If we apply the linear system of chakras to the image of a tree in the **CMLC**, Muladhara corresponds to the roots, Swadhisthana and Manipura to the trunk, and Anahata, Vishudda, Ajna, and Sahashara to the treetop, where we find expansion in symbolic ideas of leaves, flowers, fruits, and seeds. The strength of the expansion aspects of the treetop depend on the strength of the root and the structure of the trunk.

Structure, Freedom, and Connection Levels
To understand how crystals relate to the chakras in a **CMLC** perspective, in the internal geometry criterion, they are divided into three levels inspired in the vertical line of our physical bodies (the Sushumna channel) described by the Hindu chakra system. These levels are **Structure**, corresponding to functional consciousness and its predominance in the three lower chakras; **Freedom**, corresponding to the predominance of individual consciousness in the heart and throat chakras; and **Connection,** corresponding to universal consciousness and the third-eye and crown chakras.

The Structure Level aligns the three lower chakras with a specific crystal system. In a **CMLC** perspective, the root chakra is aligned with crystals from the cubic system. The sacral chakra is aligned with crystals from the orthorhombic system, and the solar plexus is aligned with crystals from the tetragonal system.

The Freedom Level corresponds to the areas of the heart and throat chakras. In a **CMLC** perspective, the heart chakra is aligned with to the monoclinic system

The Connection Level corresponds to the two upper chakras in the body. In the **CMLC** perspective, the third-eye chakra is aligned with the hexagonal system, and the crown chakra is aligned with the trigonal system.

In the color criterion, the **CMLC** uses the references of contemporary spirituality that describes the chakras system in a rainbow spectrum. The original Vedic and Yoga traditions did not describe chakras in a color spectrum. Later in the seventh and eighth century, the *Mahanirvana Tantra* attributed colors to chakras, but they were not the rainbow colors we have been training our minds to observe in the Western culture of present days (Johari, 2000; Leadbeater, 2013).

For soul-healing purposes, **The Cardinal Method of Life Connection** uses the rainbow spectrum colors in the seven vertically aligned levels of the chakras (Judith, 1987):

- The vibrational frequency of red aligns the root chakra.
- Orange balances the sacral chakra.
- Yellow balances the solar plexus.
- Green and pink balance the heart chakra.
- Turquoise blue and aqua balance the throat chakra.
- Indigo and purple balance the third-eye chakra.
- White and platinum balance the crown chakra.

Specific affirmations are the third pillar of **CMLC** crystal healing. We can find some of them published in the individual practices of the book *Your Cardinal Connections* (Ramos, 2016), and others can be prayers, mantras, sacred names, and beautiful words (such as love, life, beauty, gratitude, happiness, joy, and many others).

The **CMLC** observes three levels of energy movement that relate to the chakras and to crystals. Specific internal geometries and colors of crystals will align these specific areas. The three lower chakras (root, sacral, and solar plexus) are related to the Structure Level. The Structure Level expresses to the areas in which energy moves at a slower pace, closer to the Earth, and expresses survival, horizontal relationships, and a sense of individuality.

The **CMLC** considers the Structure Level a space related to the areas of our lives in which physical energy manifests. The root chakra, for example, located in the perineum, governs the safety of our physical body, survival, and general physical health. The sacral chakra, located in the sacral area, governs pleasure, fun, the joy of being alive, relationships, exchanges of goods, material values, and creativity. The solar plexus chakra, located on the stomach area, governs a sense of individuality, self-esteem, intelligence, knowing our place in the world, and prosperity. The Structure Level is related to a healthy sense of personal power and to joy.

The next two chakras (heart and throat) are related to the Freedom Level. The Freedom Level is related to the areas where we energy moves at a medium pace and expresses free will, and when we surrender to higher vibrational frequencies, such as love and truth, free will dives in to the will of God.

The **CMLC** considers the Freedom Level a space related to the areas of our lives in which loving energy manifests. The Freedom Level is related to a healthy sense of self-love and self-care that allows us to feel genuine love for others with respect and compassion, and unfolds in unconditional love because it comes from the truth of every living being, and from the truth of the heart.

The two upper chakras (third-eye and crown) relate to the Connection Level. The Connection Level is related to the areas in which energy moves in an even higher frequency level, at the speed closer to the reality of higher dimensions, where we are connected to higher realms and express insight, objective thinking, and divine ideas.

The **CMLC** considers the Connection Level a space related to the areas of our lives in which spiritual energy manifests. The Connection

Level is related to a healthy sense of spirituality and the accurate understanding of science, logical thinking, and geometry; and it allows us to understand with a deep and clear mind the infinite mysteries and unfolding of the world, the universe, and beyond. It brings light and meaning to life.

Crystals are used precisely to align us with the healthy manifestation of these three energy levels of consciousness related to the chakras. Their internal geometries, colors, and sounds resonate with their healthy state. With this practice, our relationships become brighter, and we keep moving forward in consciousness expansion and personal growth.

The CMLC Consciousness Levels and the Chakras
The Structure Level is related to the areas in which energy moves at a slower pace, closer to the Earth:

- The first structural level relates to interaction with the world, expressing survival, and is related to the root chakra and the cubic crystal system.
- The second structural level expresses connection with other individuals, and is associated with the sacral chakra and the orthorhombic system.
- The third structural level relates to interaction with the social environment, related to the solar plexus and the tetragonal system, and expresses mental understanding and self-esteem in a group.

The Freedom Level is related to the person's individuality in a **CMLC** perspective. In Freedom Level areas, we express our free will and not "entanglements" of collective family and cultural consciousness. The energy moves at a medium pace and expresses higher vibrational frequencies, such as love, related to the heart chakra and the monoclinic system; and truth, related to the throat chakra and the triclinic system.

The Connection Level relates to the areas in which energy moves in a higher frequency level, at the speed of thought and closer to speed of light and the reality of higher dimensions, where we are connected to higher realms and express insight and divine ideas. In a **CMLC** perspective, it expresses itself through the third-eye chakra and hexagonal system and the crown chakra with the trigonal system.

Consciousness Alignment Practice
Consciousness is everlasting, immortal, and has no beginning or end since it is beyond time and space. Since consciousness is all there is, and all existence is a multiplicity of consciousness manifestation at various levels of awareness, the **CMLC** has many practices and techniques to develop and expand individual consciousness.

The individual self and the process of self-awareness can also be called "localized consciousness" (Veltheim, 2011). As individual human beings, we hold very specific and unique experiences in our personal journeys. As self-aware beings, we can then take the next step to develop a more expanded state of being and develop cosmic consciousness.

Consciousness in a **Cardinal Method of Life Connection** perspective is literally "God Connection." Consciousness alignment is nothing more than God Connection and living constantly in the vibrations of this higher state of being.

The inner child and the ego are not by nature aligned with this God connection and expanded consciousness. On their own, without Higher Consciousness guidance, they both have a sense of omnipotence, but with different strategies. The inner child wants to control others so it can be taken care of, or fantasize about taking care of others as an unconscious way to reinforce arrogance. When the ego serves the inner child impulses, it is a processor of lower vibrational frequencies and creates separation and suffering.

The inner child has no boundaries and no discernment. Its love is immature, full of fear and attachment, and not balanced by wisdom. The ego has no boundaries and no discernment either, and since it is a processor of information coming from all areas of the psyche, it does not by nature know love or wisdom. The focus of the ego is to assert power and get things done, in a constructive way or otherwise. If the ego is being guided by benign forces, it can create many good things in the world. If other forces guide it, it will manifest itself in a distorted way through control.

The key to establishing healthy boundaries for both the inner child and the ego is through meditation and consciousness practices. The **CMLC** has several types of sessions with a practitioner, but it also has do-it-yourself techniques that can be equally powerful (such as the two practices described in the book *Your Cardinal Connections*).

When we understand the structure of **The Cardinal Method of Life Connection**, we can create energy geometries with crystals and charge them with the **CMLC** healing intentions. The **CMLC Pyramid Alignment Practice**, which is described below, is one of these techniques.

We will need three crystals and a timer for this practice. The crystals we choose will represent our mother, our father, and us. The stone to represent our mother should always be on the palm of our left hand, and our father's stone on the palm of the right hand.

Once we have done this practice a few times with the crystals in our hands, we may feel comfortable placing them next to other parts of our bodies—next to the knees, the hips, or on or next to the shoulders. Our personal crystal should be on either the forehead, the heart, the solar plexus, or the navel.

It is important to make sure we use three crystals and that they create the geometrical shape of a triangle, which is, in a three-dimensional perspective, an energetic pyramid created with three crystals.

We can find out which are the main three crystals we would like to use through intentional focus or meditation, or we can go through the crystals mentioned in this book and choose the ones that resonate best with us. It is common to feel inclined to do this practice with different crystals each time.

Now it is time to lie down, place the crystals on the palm of each hand and the third one where we intuitively feel is best, set the timer for ten minutes, relax, and allow the minutes to pass by in a calm state of consciousness.

It is very possible that a flow of information will come intuitively of things we need clarity about, or of things we were not thinking about but that may surface once we are in a state of relaxation. Thinking about our mothers and fathers and seeing what information and feelings come up may be a good starting point if we do not have any specific issue to focus on, but any kind of situation we need clarity about can be a point of focus in this practice.

We can also think about ourselves and which areas of life we are content about, and which areas need improvement. Relaxing and allowing the flow of information to expand our awareness of self in individual consciousness through this **CMLC** crystal pyramid will soon unfold into a flow of life connection.

If information does not surface immediately, giving ourselves some time to do this practice is crucial. We can also do it with three clear quartz crystals and ask for clarity and removal of obstacles to connect us to a zero-point field. The information will slowly surface with accuracy when we do the practice with clear quartz.

Ending the Journey
The Cardinal Method of Life Connection is a multidisciplinary consciousness-expansion and soul-healing modality inspired in many streams of traditional and contemporary spiritual knowledge. By associating the power of crystals with its four fundamental pillars—family constellations; Native American wisdoms; the Hindu chakras system; and recent concepts of an inner child, an ego, a real self, and a Higher Self—a structured system was created to align us with the truth and help us understand ourselves and our life processes with a deep, meaningful perspective.

The strength of the **CMLC** comes from the power of crystals. **CMLC** crystals bring awareness, truth, love, and joy to our lives. Consistent connection with these stones gradually increases our enthusiasm and joy of life, and awakens our higher levels of consciousness. This is the perfect method for those who feel drawn to crystals and are willing to engage in depth of soul, soul healing, and consciousness expansion.

Struggles with health, finances, relationships, happiness, and personal fulfillment, rigid beliefs, and limitations in general can be alleviated and may even disappear when we live from a Higher Consciousness perspective. A Higher Consciousness contemplates and integrates body, emotions, mind, spirit, and the world we live in.

I hope this journey was a life-connection experience for you and that the power of crystals brings love, joy, peace, and deeper understanding of our paths and purposes to all those who are committed to a soulful life connection.

Thank you!

REFERENCES

Barbosa, C. E. (2007). *O Livro de Ouro do Yoga*. São Paulo: Ediouro.

Calverley, R. (2013). *CHAKANA: Secret Teachings of an Ancient Andean Mystery School*. Amazon Digital Services LLC.

Castañeda, C. (1987). *The Power of Silence: Further Lessons of Don Juan*. New York, NY: Simon and Schuster.

Canato, J. (2010). *Field of Compassion; How the New Cosmology is Transforming Spiritual Life*. Sorin books, Notre Dame, Indiana.

Da Vinci, L. (2010). *The Notebooks of Leonardo da Vinci*. CreateSpace Independent Publishers.

Estés, C. P. (1997). *Women Who Run with the Wolves*. Ballantine Books.

Firace, T. (2014). *Terapêutica Imensa Vida: Uma forma de cuidar dos saudáveis*. Brasil: Tarso Firace.

Greene, L. (2000). *The Mythic Journey: The Meaning of Myth as a Guide for Life*. London, UK: Fireside; Eddison-Sadd edition.

Hall, J. (2003). *The Crystal Bible, volume 1*. Kent, OH: Walking Stick Press.

Hegel, G. W. (1977). *Phenomenology of Spirit.* Oxford University Press; Revised edition.

———. (2017). *Hegel's Philosophy of Mind.* CreateSpace Independent Publishing Platform.

Hellinger, B. (1999). *Acknowledging What Is: Conversations With Bert Hellinger.* Phoenix, AZ: Zeig, Tucker & Theisen.

———. (2012). *Ordenes Del Amor.* Barcelona: Herder Editorial.

Herrigel, E. (1999). *Zen and the Art of Archery.* New York, NY: Vintage Books.

Hobbes, T. (1994). *Leviathan.* Oxford University Press.

———. (2010). *The Elements of Law Natural and Politic.* Whitefish, MT: Kessinger Publishing Rare Reprints.

Hume, D. (1875; 1985). *Essays: Moral, Political, and Literary.* Carmel, IN: Liberty Fund; Revised edition.

Ikeda, D. (2015). *The Wisdom for Creating Happiness and Peace: Selections From the Works of Daisaku Ikeda.* Santa Monica, CA: Middleway Press.

Johari, H. (2000). *Chakras: Energy Centers of Transformation.* Rochester, Vermont: Destiny Books.

Leadbeater, C. (2013). *The Chakras.* Wheaton, IL: Quest Books.

Le Page, J. and Lilian Le Page. (2005). *Yoga Teachers' Toolbox.* Santa Rosa, CA: Integrative Yoga Therapy.

———. (n.d.). *Chakra Card Poster, Integrative Yoga Therapy.* https://iytyogatherapy.com/.

Judith, A. (1987). *Wheels of Life: A User's Guide to the Chakra System.* Woodbury, Minnesota: Llewellyn's New Age Series.

Jung C. G. (2010). *Synchronicity: An Acausal Connecting Principle.* (From Vol. 8. of the Collected Works of C. G. Jung) (Jung Extracts).

Jung C. G. (1981) *The Archetypes and The Collective Unconscious* (Collected Works of C.G. Jung Vol.9 Part 1).

Jung C. (1968) *Man and His Symbols.*

Maitri, S. (2001). *The Spiritual Dimension of the Enneagram: Nine Faces of the Soul.* New York City: TarcherPerigee.

Marin, G. (2006). *The Five Elements and The Six Conditions: A Taoist Approach to Emotional Healing, Psychology, and Internal Alchemy.* Berkeley, California: North Atlantic Books.

Pacioli, L. and Leonardo da Vinci. (2014). *De Divina Proportione (On the Divine Proportion): Facsimile in Full Color of the Original Version of 1509.* Leopold Publishing.

Palmer, H. (1991). *The Enneagram: Understanding Yourself and the Others in Our lives.* New York City: HarperOne.

Patanjali, C. E. (2015). *Os Yogasutras de Patanjali.* São Paulo: Mantra.

Pierrakos, E. (1990). *The Pathwork of Self-Transformation.* New York City: Bantam.

Pierrakos, E. and Judith Saly. (2002). *Creating Union: The Essence of Intimate Relationship (Pathwork Series).* Madison, VA: Pathwork Press.

Pierrakos, E. and Donovan Thesenga. (1993). *Fear No Evil: The Pathwork Method of Transforming the Lower Self (Pathwork Series)*. Madison, VA: Pathwork Press.

———. (1997). *Surrender to God Within: Pathwork at the Soul Level (Pathwork Series)*. Madison, VA: Pathwork Press.

Pollack, G. (2001). *Cells, Gells and the Engines of Life*. Ebner & Sons.

--------- (2013) *The Fourth Phase of Water: Beyond Solid, Liquid, and Vapor*. Ebner & Sons.

---------- (http://faculty.washington.edu/ghp/research-themes/water-science/)

Ramos, P. N. (2016). *Your Cardinal Connections: Heal Our lives, Emotions and Soul with the Power of Crystals*. CreateSpace Independent Publishing Platform.

Riso, D. H. and Russ Hudson (1999). *The Wisdom of the Enneagram: The Complete Guide to Psychological and Spiritual Growth for the Nine Personality Types*. New York, NY: Bantam.

Saint Augustine (2017). *The Magnitude of the Soul*. Amazon Digital Services, LLC.

Sams, J. (1990). *Sacred Path Cards: The Discovery of Self Through Native Teachings*. New York, NY: HarperCollins.

———. (1998). *Dancing the Dream: The Seven Sacred Paths of Human Transformation*. New York, NY: Harper-Collins.

Schneider, J. (2007). *Family Constellations: Basic Principles and Procedures.* Heidelberg, Germany: Carl Auer International.

Schumsky, S. (2003). *Exploring Chakras—Awakening Your Untapped Energy.* Wayne, NJ: New Page Books.

Sheldrake, R. (1995). *The Presence of the Past: Morphic Resonance and the Habits of Nature.* South Paris: Park Street Press.

———. (2013). *The Sense of Being Stared At: And Other Unexplained Powers of Human Minds.* South Paris: Park Street Press.

--------- (http://www.co-intelligence.org/P-morphogeneticfields.html)

Spiller, J. (1997). *Astrology for the Soul.* New York, NY: Bantam.

Thesenga, S. (2001). *The Undefended Self: Living the Pathwork.* Madison, VA: Pathwork Press.

Thomas, A. (2008). *The Gemstones Handbook (Properties, Identification and Use).* London: New Holland Publishers.

Tolle, E. (2008). *A New Earth: Awakening to Your Life's Purpose.* London, UK: Penguin.

Torra, M. (2014). *Incan Anatomy of the Soul.* Victoria, Australia: Chakana Creations.

Veltheim, J. (2011). *PaRama BodyTalk, Unit 1.* Sarasota, FL: International BodyTalk Association.

Veltheim, J. and S. Muiznieks. (2013). *BodyTalk Fundamentals.* Sarasota, FL: PaRama LLC.

Vitale, D. J. (2013). *At Zero: The Final Secrets to "Zero Limits" The Quest for Miracles Through Ho'oponopono*. Hoboken, NJ: John Wiley & Sons, Inc.

Vitale, J. and I. H. Len. (2008). *Zero Limits: The Secret Hawaiian System for Wealth, Health, Peace, and More*. Hoboken, NJ: John Wiley & Sons, Inc.

Wood, C. C. (2004). *Opening to Abundance*. Charlottesville, VA: Pathwork Press.

Made in the USA
Columbia, SC
08 August 2017